*A Collection of
Writings Related to
Occult, Esoteric,
Rosicrucian and
Hermetic Literature,
Including Freemasonry,
the Kabbalah, the Tarot,
Alchemy and Theosophy*

Volume 1

Other Books in this Series and Related Titles

Magical Essays and Instructions by Florence Farr
(978-1-63118-418-5)

Ancient Mysteries and Secret Societies by Manly P. Hall
(978-1-63118-410-9)

The First and Second Gospels of the Infancy of Jesus Christ
by Thomas and James (978-1-63118-415-4)

The Book of the Watchers by Enoch
(978-1-63118-416-1)

The Human Aura: Astral Colors and Thought Forms
by Swami Panchadasi and William Walker Atkinson
(978-1-63118-419-2)

Rosa Alchemica, The Tables of Law & The Adoration of the Magi
by William Butler Yeats (978-1-63118-421-5)

The Feminine Occult by various authors
(978-1-63118-711-7)

Occult Symbolism of Animals, Insects, Reptiles, Fish and Birds
by Manly P. Hall (978-1-63118-420-8)

The Lives of Adam and Eve by Moses
(978-1-63118-414-7)

A Collection of Writings Related to Occult, Esoteric, Rosicrucian and Hermetic Literature, Including Freemasonry, the Kabbalah, the Tarot, Alchemy and Theosophy various authors *Volumes 1-4*
(978-1-63118-713-1) (978-1-63118-714-8)
(978-1-63118-715-5) (978-1-63118-716-2)

Audio Versions are also Available on Audible and iTunes

A Collection of Writings Related to Occult, Esoteric, Rosicrucian and Hermetic Literature, Including Freemasonry, the Kabbalah, the Tarot, Alchemy and Theosophy

Volume 1

By

Manly P. Hall, William Butler Yeats, Helena P. Blavatsky, Pythagoras, Paracelsus, Arthur Edward Waite, Isaac Newton, Eliphas Levi, William Wynn Westcott, L. W. de Laurence, Max Heindel, Jules Doinel, C. W. Leadbeater, P. D. Ouspensky, Jerome A. Anderson and Albert G. Mackey

Copyright © 2019 Lamp of Trismegistus. All rights reserved. No part of this publication may be reproduced or transmitted in any form or by any means, electronic or mechanical, including photocopying, recording, or by any information storage and retrieval system, without permission in writing from Lamp of Trismegistus. Reviewers may quote brief passages.

ISBN: 978-1-63118-713-1

Table of Contents

Introduction…7

The Human Body in Symbolism
by Manly P. Hall…9

The Body of Father Christian Rosencreutz
by William Butler Yeats…27

The Kabbalah of Masonry
by William Wynn Westcott…29

Spiritual Progress
by Helena P. Blavatsky…43

The Treasure of Treasures for Alchemists
by Paracelsus…47

Instructions on Crystal Gazing
by L. W. de Laurence…57

Mystical Realization
by Arthur Edward Waite…63

Keynote of the Rosicrucian Teachings
by Max Heindel…71

The Magical Evocation of Apollonius of Tyana
by Eliphas Levi…75

Simon Magus
by Jules Doinel…85

The Emerald Tablet
by Isaac Newton...95

The Reality of the Astral Plane
by C. W. Leadbeater...97

What is Tarot?
by P. D. Ouspensky...129

The Importance of Ceremonial Magic
by Arthur Edward Waite...141

The Golden Verses of Pythagoras
by Pythagoras...151

The Legend of the Holy Grail and its Connection with Templars and Freemasons
by Arthur Edward Waite...157

Alchemy of the Rosicrucians
by Jerome A. Anderson...185

Initiation, the Ancient Mysteries and the Dionysiac Artificers
by Albert G. Mackey...189

Introduction

Presented here is a collection of essays on a variety of related subjects, for students of the Esoteric sciences.

The word "esoteric" can be difficult to define. Esotericism in general can be seen less as a system of beliefs and more as a category, which encompasses numerous, different systems of beliefs. It's a bit of juxtaposition, since the word "esoteric" indicates something that few people know about, while the term itself broadly covers numerous philosophies, practices, areas of study and belief systems.

In a greater sense, Esotericism acts as a storehouse for secret knowledge, which is often considered ancient (by *tradition, if not by fact)*, passed down from generation to generation, in private. At various times in history, simply possessing the knowledge of some of these subjects, was considered illegal and a jailable offence, if discovered. This usually included such general topics as Alchemy, Qabalah, Hermeticism, Occultism, Ceremonial Magic, Astrology, Divination, Rosicrucianism and so on. Collectively, these areas of study were often referred to as the esoteric sciences.

Sometimes, the outer garment of a subject isn't esoteric, while what is hidden beneath it, is. As an example, Freemasonry isn't necessarily esoteric by nature (at *least not anymore)*, but certain signs, passwords and handshakes given to the candidate during their initiation, are in fact, esoteric, in the sense that they are hidden from the general public.

Today, in the twenty-first century, such topics are readily available at bookstores across the country, and numerous mainsteam publishers offer beginners guides and coffee-table volumes on many of these subjects, intended for mass appeal. Books like "The Secret" have turned previously arcane topics into household knowledge. All that being the case, however, it isn't to say that there still aren't buried secrets to uncover, ancient wisdom being ignored and forgotten mysteries to be explored. In fact, it is often that we are only able to further our own studies by standing on the shoulders of these disappearing giants.

Lamp of Trismegistus is doing its part to help preserve humanity's esoteric history by making some of these classics available to those students who are seeking to unearth the knowledge of these ancient colossi.

So, be sure to check other titles from our *Esoteric Classics* series, as well as our *Occult Fiction, Theosophical Classics, Foundations of Freemasonry* and our *Christian Apocrypha Series*. You can also download the audio versions of most of these titles from iTunes or Audible, for learning on the go.

The Human Body in Symbolism

by Manly P. Hall

The oldest, the most profound, the most universal of all symbols is the human body. The Greeks, Persians, Egyptians, and Hindus considered a philosophical analysis of man's triune nature to be an indispensable part of ethical and religious training. The Mysteries of every nation taught that the laws, elements, and powers of the universe were epitomized in the human constitution; that everything which existed outside of man had its analogue within man. The universe, being immeasurable in its immensity and inconceivable in its profundity, was beyond mortal estimation. Even the gods themselves could comprehend but a part of the inaccessible glory which was their source. When temporarily permeated with divine enthusiasm, man may transcend for a brief moment the limitations of his own personality and behold in part that celestial effulgence in which all creation is bathed. But even in his periods of greatest illumination man is incapable of imprinting upon the substance of his rational soul a perfect image of the multiform expression of celestial activity.

Recognizing the futility of attempting to cope intellectually with that which transcends the comprehension of the rational faculties, the early philosophers turned their attention from the inconceivable Divinity to man himself, within the narrow confines of whose nature they found manifested all the mysteries of the external spheres. As the natural outgrowth of this practice there was fabricated a secret theological system in which God was considered as the Grand

Man and, conversely, man as the little god. Continuing this analogy, the universe was regarded as a man and, conversely, man as a miniature universe. The greater universe was termed the *Macrocosm*--the Great World or Body--and the Divine Life or spiritual entity controlling its functions was called the *Macroprosophus*. Man's body, or the individual human universe, was termed the *Microcosm*, and the Divine Life or spiritual entity controlling its functions was called the *Microprosophus*. The pagan Mysteries were primarily concerned with instructing neophytes in the true relationship existing between the *Macrocosm* and the *Microcosm*--in other words, between God and man. Accordingly, the key to these analogies between the organs and functions of the *Microcosmic* man and those of the *Macrocosmic* Man constituted the most prized possession of the early initiates.

In *Isis Unveiled*, H. P. Blavatsky summarizes the pagan concept of man as follows:

> "Man is a little world--a microcosm inside the great universe. Like a fetus, he is suspended, by all his *three* spirits, in the matrix of the macrocosmos; and while his terrestrial body is in constant sympathy with its parent earth, his astral soul lives in unison with the sidereal *anima mundi*. He is in it, as it is in him, for the world-pervading element fills all space, and is space itself, only shoreless and infinite. As to his third spirit, the divine, what is it but an infinitesimal ray, one of the countless radiations proceeding directly from the Highest Cause-- the Spiritual Light of the World? This is the trinity of organic and inorganic nature--the spiritual and the physical, which are three in one, and of which Proclus says that 'The first monad is the Eternal God; the second, eternity; the third, the paradigm, or pattern of

the universe;' the three constituting the Intelligible Triad."

Long before the introduction of idolatry into religion, the early priests caused the statue of a man to be placed in the sanctuary of the temple. This human figure symbolized the Divine Power in all its intricate manifestations. Thus the priests of antiquity accepted man as their textbook, and through the study of him learned to understand the greater and more abstruse mysteries of the celestial scheme of which they were a part. It is not improbable that this mysterious figure standing over the primitive altars was made in the nature of a manikin and, like certain emblematic hands in the Mystery schools, was covered with either carved or painted hieroglyphs. The statue may have opened, thus showing the relative positions of the organs, bones, muscles, nerves, and other parts. After ages of research, the manikin became a mass of intricate hieroglyphs and symbolic figures. Every part had its secret meaning. The measurements formed a basic standard by means of which it was possible to measure all parts of cosmos. It was a glorious composite emblem of all the knowledge possessed by the sages and hierophants.

Then came the age of idolatry. The Mysteries decayed from within. The secrets were lost and none knew the identity of the mysterious man who stood over the altar. It was remembered only that the figure was a sacred and glorious symbol of the Universal Power, and it finally came to be looked upon as a god--the One in whose image man was made. Having lost the knowledge of the purpose for which the manikin was originally constructed, the priests worshiped this effigy until at last their lack of spiritual understanding brought the temple down in ruins about their heads and the statue crumbled with the civilization that had forgotten its meaning.

Proceeding from this assumption of the first theologians that man is actually fashioned in the image of God, the initiated minds of past ages erected the stupendous structure of theology upon the foundation of the human body. The religious world of today is almost totally ignorant of the fact that the science of biology is the fountainhead of its doctrines and tenets. Many of the codes and laws believed by modern divines to have been direct revelations from Divinity are in reality the fruitage of ages of patient delving into the intricacies of the human constitution and the infinite wonders revealed by such a study.

In nearly all the sacred books of the world can be traced an anatomical analogy. This is most evident in their creation myths. Anyone familiar with embryology and obstetrics will have no difficulty in recognizing the basis of the allegory concerning Adam and Eve and the Garden of Eden, the nine degrees of the Eleusinian Mysteries, and the Brahmanic legend of Vishnu's incarnations. The story of the Universal Egg, the Scandinavian myth of Ginnungagap (*the dark cleft in space in which the seed of the world is sown*), and the use of the fish as the emblem of the paternal generative power--all show the true origin of theological speculation. The philosophers of antiquity realized that man himself was the key to the riddle of life, for he was the living image of the Divine Plan, and in future ages humanity also will come to realize more fully the solemn import of those ancient words: "The proper study of mankind is man."

Both God and man have a twofold constitution, of which the superior part is invisible and the inferior visible. In both there is also an intermediary sphere, marking the point where these visible and invisible natures meet. As the spiritual nature of God controls His objective universal form-which is actually a crystallized idea--so the spiritual nature of man is the invisible cause and controlling power of his visible material personality. Thus it is evident that the spirit of man bears the same relationship to his material body that God bears to the objective universe. The Mysteries taught that spirit, or life, was anterior to form and that what is anterior includes all that is posterior to itself. Spirit being anterior to form, form is therefore included within the realm of spirit. It is also a popular statement or belief that man's spirit is within his body. According to the conclusions of philosophy and theology, however, this belief is erroneous, for spirit first circumscribes an area and then manifests within it. Philosophically speaking, form, being a part of spirit, is within spirit; but: spirit is more than the sum of form, As the material nature of man is therefore within the sum of spirit, so the Universal Nature, including the entire sidereal system, is within the all-pervading essence of God--the Universal Spirit.

According to another concept of the ancient wisdom, all bodies--whether spiritual or material--have three centers, called by the Greeks the *upper* center, the *middle* center, and the *lower* center. An apparent ambiguity will here be noted. To diagram or symbolize adequately abstract mental verities is impossible, for the diagrammatic representation of one aspect of metaphysical relationships may be an actual contradiction of some other aspect. While that which is above is generally considered superior in dignity and power, in reality that which is in the center is superior and anterior to both that which is said to be above and that which is said to be below. Therefore, it must be said that the first--which is considered as being above--is actually in the center, while both of the others (which are said to be either above or below) are actually beneath. This point can be further simplified if the reader will consider *above* as indicating degree of proximity to source and *below* as indicating degree of distance from source, source being posited in the actual center and relative distance being the various points along the radii from the center toward the circumference. In matters pertaining to philosophy and theology, *up* may be considered as toward the center and *down* as toward the circumference. Center is spirit; circumference is matter. Therefore, *up* is toward spirit along an ascending scale of spirituality; *down* is toward matter along an ascending scale of materiality. The latter concept is partly expressed by the apex of a cone which, when viewed from above, is seen as a point in the exact center of the circumference formed by the base of the cone.

These three universal centers--the one above, the one below, and the link uniting them-represent three suns or three aspects of one sun--centers of effulgence. These also have their analogues in the three grand centers of the human body, which, like the physical universe, is a Demiurgic fabrication. "The first of these suns," says Thomas Taylor, "is analogous to light when viewed subsisting in its fountain the sun; the second to the light immediately proceeding from the sun; and the third to the splendor communicated to other natures by this light."

Since the superior (or spiritual) center is in the midst of the other two, its analogue in the physical body is the heart-- the most spiritual and mysterious organ in the human body. The second center (or the link between the superior and inferior worlds) is elevated to the position of greatest physical dignity--the brain. The third (or lower) center is relegated to the position of least physical dignity but greatest physical importance--the generative system. Thus the heart is symbolically the source of life; the brain the link by which, through rational intelligence, life and form are united; and the generative system--or infernal creator--the source of that power by which physical organisms are produced. The ideals and aspirations of the individual depend largely upon which of these three centers of power predominates in scope and activity of expression. In the materialist the lower center is the strongest, in the intellectualist the higher center; but in the initiate the middle center--by bathing the two extremes in a flood of spiritual effulgence--controls wholesomely both the mind and the body.

As light bears witness of life-which is its source-so the mind bears witness of the spirit, and activity in a still lower plane bears witness of intelligence. Thus the mind bears witness of the heart, while the generative system, in turn, bears witness of the mind. Accordingly, the spiritual nature is most commonly symbolized by a heart; the intellectual power by an opened eye, symbolizing the pineal gland or Cyclopean eye, which is the two-faced Janus of the pagan Mysteries; and the generative system by a flower, a staff, a cup, or a hand.

While all the Mysteries recognized the heart as the center of spiritual consciousness, they often purposely ignored this concept and used the heart in its exoteric sense as the symbol of the emotional nature, In this arrangement the generative center represented the physical body, the heart the emotional body, and the brain the mental body. The brain represented the superior sphere, but after the initiates had passed through the lower degrees they were instructed that the brain was the proxy of the spiritual flame dwelling in the innermost recesses of the heart. The student of esotericism discovers ere long that the ancients often resorted to various blinds to conceal the true interpretations of their Mysteries. The substitution of the brain for the heart was one of these blinds.

The three degrees of the ancient Mysteries were, with few exceptions, given in chambers which represented the three great centers of the human and Universal bodies. If possible, the temple itself was constructed in the form of the human body. The candidate entered between the feet and received the highest degree in the point corresponding to the brain. Thus the first degree was the material mystery and its symbol was the generative system; it raised the candidate through the various degrees of concrete thought. The second degree was given in the chamber corresponding to the heart, but represented the middle power which was the mental link. Here the candidate was initiated into the mysteries of abstract thought and lifted as high as the mind was capable of penetrating. He then passed into the third chamber, which, analogous to the brain, occupied the highest position in the temple but, analogous to the heart, was of the greatest dignity. In the brain chamber the heart mystery was given. Here the initiate for the first time truly comprehended the meaning of those immortal words: "As a man thinketh in his heart, so is he." As there are seven hearts in the brain so there are seven brains in the heart, but this is a matter of superphysics of which little can be said at the present time.

Proclus writes on this subject in the first book of *On the Theology of Plato*:

> "Indeed, Socrates in the (First) Alcibiades rightly observes, that the soul entering into herself will behold all other things, and deity itself. For verging to her own union, and to the center of all life, laying aside multitude, and the variety of the all manifold powers which she contains, she ascends to the highest watch-tower offerings. And as in the most holy of the mysteries, they say, that the mystics at first meet with the multi form, and many-shaped genera, which are hurled forth before the gods, but on entering the temple, unmoved, and guarded by the mystic rites, they genuinely receive in

their heart, divine illumination, and divested of their garments, as they would say, participate of a divine nature; the same mode, as it appears to me, takes place in the speculation of wholes. For the soul when looking at things posterior to herself, beholds the shadows and images of beings, but when she converts herself to herself she evolves her own essence, and the reasons which she contains. And at first indeed, she only as it were beholds herself; but, when she penetrates more profoundly into the knowledge of herself, she finds in herself both intellect, and the orders of beings. When however, she proceeds into her interior recesses, and into the adytum as it were of the soul, she perceives with her eye closed (without the aid of the lower mind), the genus of the gods, and the unities of beings. For all things are in us psychically, and through this we are naturally capable of knowing all things, by exciting the powers and the images of wholes which we contain."

The initiates of old warned their disciples that an image is not a reality but merely the objectification of a subjective idea. The image of the gods were not designed to be objects of worship but were to be regarded merely as emblems or reminders of invisible powers and principles. Similarly, the body of man must not be considered as the individual but only as the house of the individual, in the same manner that the temple was the House of God. In a state of grossness and perversion man's body is the tomb or prison of a divine principle; in a state of unfoldment and regeneration it is the House or Sanctuary of the Deity by whose creative powers it was fashioned. "Personality is suspended upon a thread from the nature of Being," declares the secret work. Man is essentially a permanent and immortal principle; only his bodies pass through the cycle of birth and death. The immortal is the reality; the mortal is the unreality. During each period of earth life, reality thus dwells in unreality, to be liberated from it temporarily by death and permanently by illumination.

While generally regarded as polytheists, the pagans gained this reputation not because they worshiped more than one God but rather because they personified the attributes of this God, thereby creating a pantheon of posterior deities each manifesting a part of what the One God manifested as a whole. The various pantheons of ancient religions therefore actually represent the catalogued and personified attributes of Deity. In this respect they correspond to the hierarchies of the Hebrew Qabbalists. All the gods and goddesses of antiquity consequently have their analogies in the human body, as have also the elements, planets, and constellations which were assigned as proper vehicles for these celestials. Four body centers are assigned to the elements, the seven vital organs to the planets, the twelve principal parts and members to the zodiac, the invisible parts of man's divine nature to various supermundane deities, while the hidden God was declared to manifest through the marrow in the bones.

It is difficult for many to realize that they are actual universes; that their physical bodies are a visible nature through the structure of which countless waves of evolving life are unfolding their latent potentialities. Yet through man's physical body not only are a mineral, a plant, and an animal kingdom evolving, but also unknown classifications and divisions of invisible spiritual life. Just as cells are infinitesimal units in the structure of man, so man is an infinitesimal unit in the structure of the universe. A theology based upon the knowledge and appreciation of these relationships is as profoundly just as it is profoundly true.

As man's physical body has five distinct and important extremities--two legs, two arms, and a head, of which the last governs the first four--the number 5 has been accepted as the symbol of man. By its four corners the pyramid symbolizes the arms and legs, and by its apex the head, thus indicating that one rational power controls four irrational corners. The hands and feet are used to represent the four elements, of which the two feet are earth and water, and the two hands fire and air. The brain then symbolizes the sacred fifth element--æther--which controls and unites the other four. If the feet are placed together and the arms outspread, man then symbolizes the cross with the rational intellect as the head or upper limb.

The fingers and toes also have special significance. The toes represent the Ten Commandments of the physical law and the fingers the Ten Commandments of the spiritual law. The four fingers of each hand represent the four elements and the three phalanges of each finger represent the divisions of the element, so that in each hand there are twelve parts to the fingers, which are analogous to the signs of the zodiac, whereas the two phalanges and base of each thumb signify the threefold Deity. The first phalange corresponds to the creative aspect, the second to the preservative aspect, and the base to the generative and destructive aspect. When the hands are brought together, the result is the twenty-four Elders and the six Days of Creation.

In symbolism the body is divided vertically into halves, the right half being considered as light and the left half as darkness. By those unacquainted with the true meanings of light and darkness the light half was denominated spiritual and the left half material. Light is the symbol of objectivity; darkness of subjectivity. Light is a manifestation of life and is therefore posterior to life. That which is anterior to light is darkness, in which light exists temporarily but darkness permanently. As life precedes light, its only symbol is darkness, and darkness is considered as the veil which must eternally conceal the true nature of abstract and undifferentiated Being.

In ancient times men fought with their right arms and defended the vital centers with their left arms, on which was carried the protecting shield. The right half of the body was regarded therefore as offensive and the left half defensive. For this reason also the right side of the body was considered masculine and the left side feminine. Several authorities are of the opinion that the present prevalent right-handedness of the race is the outgrowth of the custom of holding the left hand in restraint for defensive purposes. Furthermore, as the source of Being is in the primal darkness which preceded light, so the spiritual nature of man is in the dark part of his being, for the heart is on the left side.

Among the curious misconceptions arising from the false practice of associating darkness with evil is one by which several early nations used the right hand for all constructive labors and the left hand for only those purposes termed unclean and unfit for the sight of the gods. For the same reason black magic was often referred to as the left-hand path, and heaven was said to be upon the right and hell upon the left. Some philosophers further declared that there were two methods of writing: one from left to right, which was considered the exoteric method; the other from right to left, which was considered esoteric. The exoteric writing was that which was done out or away from the heart, while the esoteric writing was that which--like the ancient Hebrew--was written toward the heart.

The secret doctrine declares that every part and member

of the body is epitomized in the brain and, in turn, that all that is in the brain is epitomized in the heart. In symbolism the human head is frequently used to represent intelligence and self-knowledge. As the human body in its entirety is the most perfect known product of the earth's evolution, it was employed to represent Divinity--the highest appreciable state or condition. Artists, attempting to portray Divinity, often show only a hand emerging from an impenetrable cloud. The cloud signifies the Unknowable Divinity concealed from man by human limitation. The hand signifies the Divine activity, the only part of God which is cognizable to the lower senses.

The face consists of a natural trinity: the eyes representing the spiritual power which comprehends; the nostrils representing the preservative and vivifying power; and the mouth and ears representing the material Demiurgic power of the lower world. The first sphere is eternally existent and is creative; the second sphere pertains to the mystery of the creative breach; and the third sphere to the creative word. By the Word of God the material universe was fabricated, and the seven creative powers, or vowel sounds--which had been brought into existence by the speaking of the Word--became the seven Elohim or Deities by whose power and ministration the lower world was organized. Occasionally the Deity is symbolized by an eye, an ear, a nose, or a mouth. By the first, Divine awareness is signified; by the second, Divine interest; by the third, Divine vitality; and by the fourth, Divine command.

The ancients did not believe that spirituality made men either righteous or rational, but rather that righteousness and rationality made men spiritual. The Mysteries taught that spiritual illumination was attained only by bringing the lower nature up to a certain standard of efficiency and purity. The Mysteries were therefore established for the purpose of unfolding the nature of man according to certain fixed rules which, when faithfully followed, elevated the human consciousness to a point where it was capable of cognizing its own constitution and the true purpose of existence. This knowledge of how man's manifold constitution could be most quickly and most completely regenerated to the point of spiritual illumination constituted the secret, or esoteric, doctrine of antiquity. Certain apparently physical organs and centers are in reality the veils or sheaths of spiritual centers. What these were and how they could be unfolded was never revealed to the unregenerate, for the philosophers realized that once he understands the complete working of any system, a man may accomplish a prescribed end without being qualified to manipulate and control the effects which he has produced. For this reason long periods of probation were imposed, so that the knowledge of how to become as the gods might remain the sole possession of the worthy.

Lest that knowledge be lost, however, it was concealed in allegories and myths which were meaningless to the profane but self-evident to those acquainted with that theory of personal redemption which was the foundation of philosophical theology. Christianity itself may be cited as an example. The entire New Testament is in fact an ingeniously concealed exposition of the secret processes of human regeneration. The characters so long considered as historical men and women are really the personification of certain processes which take place in the human body when man begins the task of consciously liberating himself from the bondage of ignorance and death.

The garments and ornamentations supposedly worn by the gods are also keys, for in the Mysteries clothing was considered as synonymous with form. The degree of spirituality or materiality of the organisms was signified by the quality, beauty, and value of the garments worn. Man's physical body was looked upon as the robe of his spiritual nature; consequently, the more developed were his super-substantial powers the more glorious his apparel. Of course, clothing was originally worn for ornamentation rather than protection, and such practice still prevails among many primitive peoples. The Mysteries caught that man's only lasting adornments were his virtues and worthy characteristics; that he was clothed in his own accomplishments and adorned by his attainments. Thus the white robe was symbolic of purity, the red robe of sacrifice and love, and the blue robe of altruism and integrity. Since the body was said to be the robe of the spirit, mental or moral deformities were depicted as deformities of the body.

Considering man's body as the measuring rule of the universe, the philosophers declared that all things resemble in constitution--if not in form--the human body. The Greeks, for example, declared Delphi to be the navel of the earth, for the physical planet was looked upon as a gigantic human being twisted into the form of a ball. In contradistinction to the belief of Christendom that the earth is an inanimate thing, the pagans considered not only the earth but also all the sidereal bodies as individual creatures possessing individual intelligences. They even went so far as to view the various kingdoms of Nature as individual entities. The animal kingdom, for example, was looked upon as one being--a composite of all the creatures composing that kingdom. This prototypic beast was a mosaic embodiment of all animal propensities and within its nature the entire animal world existed as the human species exists within the constitution of the prototypic Adam.

In the same manner, races, nations, tribes, religions, states, communities, and cities were viewed as composite entities, each made up of varying numbers of individual units. Every community has an individuality which is the sum of the individual attitudes of its inhabitants. Every religion is an individual whose body is made up of a hierarchy and vast host of individual worshipers. The organization of any religion represents its physical body, and its individual members the cell life making up this organism. Accordingly, religions, races, and communities--like individuals--pass through Shakespeare's *Seven Ages*, for the life of man is a standard by which the perpetuity of all things is estimated.

    According to the secret doctrine, man, through the gradual refinement of his vehicles and the ever-increasing sensitiveness resulting from that refinement, is gradually overcoming the limitations of matter and is disentangling himself from his mortal coil. When humanity has completed its physical evolution, the empty shell of materiality left behind will be used by other life waves as steppingstones to their own liberation. The trend of man's evolutionary growth is ever toward his own essential Selfhood. At the point of deepest materialism, therefore, man is at the greatest distance from Himself. According to the Mystery teachings, not all the spiritual nature of man incarnates in matter. The spirit of man is diagrammatically shown as an equilateral triangle with one point downward. This lower point, which is one-third of the spiritual nature but in comparison to the dignity of the other two is much less than a third, descends into the illusion of material existence for a brief space of time. That which never clothes itself in the sheath of matter is the Hermetic *Anthropos*--the Overman-- analogous to the Cyclops or guardian *dæmon* of the Greeks, the *angel* of Jakob Böhme, and the Oversoul of Emerson, "that Unity, that Oversoul, within which every man's particular being is contained and made one with all other."

At birth only a third part of the Divine Nature of man temporarily dissociates itself from its own immortality and takes upon itself the dream of physical birth and existence, animating with its own celestial enthusiasm a vehicle composed of material elements, part of and bound to the material sphere. At death this incarnated part awakens from the dream of physical existence and reunites itself once more with its eternal condition. This periodical descent of spirit into matter is termed the *wheel of life and death*, and the principles involved are treated at length by the philosophers under the subject of metempsychosis. By initiation into the Mysteries and a certain process known as operative theology, this law of birth and death is transcended, and during the course of physical existence that part of the spirit which is asleep in form is awakened without the intervention of death--the inevitable Initiator--and is consciously reunited with the *Anthropos*, or the overshadowing substance of itself. This is at once the primary purpose and the consummate achievement of the Mysteries: that man shall become aware of and consciously be reunited with the divine source of himself without tasting of physical dissolution.

The Body of Father Christian Rosencrux

by William Butler Yeats

The followers of the Father Christian Rosencrux, says the old tradition, wrapped his imperishable body in noble raiment and laid it under the house of their order, in a tomb containing the symbols of all things in heaven and earth, and in the waters under the earth, and set about him inextinguishable magical lamps, which burnt on generation after generation, until other students of the order came upon the tomb by chance. It seems to me that the imagination has had no very different history during the last two hundred years, but has been laid in a great tomb of criticism, and had set over it inextinguishable magical lamps of wisdom and romance, and has been altogether so nobly housed and appareled that we have forgotten that its wizard lips are closed, or but opened for the complaining of some melancholy and ghostly voice. The ancients and the Elizabethans abandoned themselves to imagination as a woman abandons herself to love, and created great beings who made the people of this world seem but shadows, and great passions which made our loves and hatreds appear but ephemeral and trivial phantasies; but now it is not the great persons, or the great passions we imagine, which absorb us, for the persons and passions in our poems are mainly reflections our mirror has caught from older poems or from the life about us, but the wise comments we make upon them, the criticism of life we wring from their fortunes. Arthur and his Court are nothing, but the many-colored lights that play about them are as beautiful as the lights from cathedral windows; Pompilia and Guido are but little, while the ever-recurring meditations and expositions which climax in the mouth of the Pope are among the wisest of the Christian age. I cannot get it out of my mind that this age of criticism is about to pass, and an age of imagination, of emotion, of moods, of revelation, about to come in its place; for certainly belief in a super-sensual world is at hand again; and when the notion that we are 'phantoms of the earth and water' has gone down the wind, we will trust our own being and all it desires to invent; and when the external world is no more the standard of reality, we will learn again that the great Passions are angels of God, and that to embody them 'uncurbed in their eternal glory,' even in their labor for the ending of man's peace and prosperity, is more than to comment, however wisely, upon the tendencies of our time, or to express the socialistic, or humanitarian, or other forces of our time, or even 'to sum up' our time, as the phrase is; for Art is a revelation, and not a criticism, and the life of the artist is in the old saying, 'The wind bloweth where it listeth, and thou hearest the sound thereof, but canst not tell whence it cometh and whither it goeth; so is every one that is born of the spirit.'

The Kabbalah of Masonry

by William Wynn Westcott

Freemasonry, our English Craft, describes itself as a "system of morality veiled in allegory, and illustrated by symbols." A little consideration will, I feel sure, convince us that it is something more than this.

'Tis not the whole of life to live, Nor all of death to die,'

wrote the poet Montgomery, and the aphorism is applicable also to Freemasonry.

Our Ritual presents us with ample internal evidence that the mystery of the Craft lies deeper than a mere scheme of moral maxims. Our Ritual contains distinct prayers, addressed to the clearly defined one God; the Unity of the God we address is the essence of his type.

Our Ritual includes several most serious obligations. To what? To morality? No, to secrecy. These obligations are taken subject to certain penalties. What penalties? Fine? Or seclusion? No, to penalties of whose nature we are all aware and which I need not therefore particularize.

Can any rational man believe that such formulae were originally designed for the purpose of veiling a scheme of morality; a system of morals suitable to all men, whose realization would be the achievement of earthly perfection? Our Ritual embodies and traces out a definite legend, or set of legends, it insists on the acceptance of these events as positive truth, wholly apart from any evidence from common history.

Nay, even in spite of it. These events must be grasped by the perfect mason as masonic truth, and not believed only, but personally acted. Could such an unusual, not to say unnatural, claim on a man be made simply to veil a moral precept? Could such a state of mind and body be made peremptory simply to paint a beautiful allegory?

Our mysteries are positively guarded by signs, tokens, and words, so stringently accorded and so carefully preserved, the profane are clearly convinced that even the most apparently reliable exposés of them are but make-believes. If these secret modes of recognizable shrouded but a scheme to make men more honest, or more charitable, is it reasonable to suppose that this sanctity would have grown up around them?

No, my brethren, it would have been but a vain and foolish association which should have been created to make a secret of morality.

Freemasonry, then, must be something more, much more. To us, the representatives of the Freemasonry of today it may be but a light thing, and I fear it often is. But let us remember our great claim, the early original of our Order, there must be our hunting ground for the cause of our secrecy, for the constitution of the Fraternity, for the intense obligations imposed on each one of us.

And now I should ask each of you what is the greatest aim of an earthly existence? Is it not to prepare for another? Do we not all feel assured that, we must come to an end of this terrene existence? Do we not feel that the "I," the "Ego" within each one of us cannot end with this world? *"To sleep, to die, perchance to dream; ay, there's the rub."*

The aim of each mortal, then, is to grasp at an ideal life, to prepare for another stage of existence; and how? How but through one's Creator? Who else could make or mar my life-but I and my Creator? Religion is the name we mortals give to our aspirations towards our Creator, and to our schemes to read Him.

Religion, then, is the key to try in this secret lock; a secret religion might need hiding, what from? Whom from? From one's Creator? No; from one's fellow man, who in time past as far as history can reach, has never failed to sully the face of this fair earth with blasphemies, with idolatry, with persecutions, with religious martyrdom. Religious zeal and intolerance have been too often but convertible terms.

To combat the risk of death what weapon should we expect to find chosen? What but, the threat of death? Not a perfect weapon possibly, not an ideally perfect one, not a heavenly one; but one applicable and competent to protect against evil doers.

Now Freemasonry has, it has appeared, a grand central idea, a creator, a One God. Does history give us any record that the holders of such a dogma have been the mass of the inhabitants, or the greatest men throughout the world, or throughout the centuries? Or does history show us that believers in a unique impersonal Deity, pure and undefiled, not consenting unto iniquity, have ever been aught but a minority, often persecuted, and always reviled? The minority has doubtless been a growing one, and has of late been too important to be crushed by threats of death, and in a parallel mode we now find as I pointed out at first we have even arrived at the stage of having forgotten why our obligations were designed.

Such, my brethren, is the suggestion of my theme; our present system of allegorical morality is the lineal descendant of true veiled Monotheism, which in a pagan and persecuting world had need in every clime and in every age of some scheme of self-defense.

We may not be able to trace in definite order every step in the vast procession of forms through which the Monotheistic secret has been shrouded, veiled, and preserved, or even to trace a distinct groove in the wheel of time in any one nation or century, but history is at no time free from the survival of scraps of evidence that a mystic association was at work, preserving and consecrating some high ideal, some great dogma.

The absence of distinct and definite histories of secret Monotheistic societies is really an evidence of their reality and of their successful operation, and the vast number of forms assumed by the true Believers, at one time resembling a military organization, at another a priesthood, at another a philosophic sect, at another time the secret held by three, two, or even one man—a king—at others of wide-spread significance, is to me but evidence of the reality of my contention.

And I affirm, and could afford considerable evidence in support of the view that even among the priesthood of what have apparently been the most debased and extravagant religions, there has always existed an esoteric doctrine held by a select hierarchy, and that doctrine the Unity of God, as a Creator, Designer, and Ruler, apart from the modes of His manifestation to us mortals, whether by processes and sublime emanations, or by Sonship, or by influence of the Holy Spirit, or by the development in sex, or by maternity; all of these modes of representing the action of a unique impersonal God, in relation to His works.

The Jews have ever been true Monotheists and have been ever persecuted, and the Old Testament, their own narrative of themselves, is perhaps the chief extant volume recording struggles to preserve a pure Theocracy, to preserve a religion of Monotheism, pure and free from idolatry. And although at times we find, superficially speaking, the whole Jewish nation gone astray, yet there is collateral evidence that there were at every epoch some true believers.

As the Jewish power declined, and at length fell, pure Monotheism trembled, and had to shroud its head for a long period from the dominant pagan conqueror. Hence arose one series of secret associations which has extended down to our own times, and whose development is now in our midst as Freemasonry, to me the lineal descendant of the early schemes and associations designed to perpetuate a pure religion and a corresponding system of moral ethics.

Our secret brotherhood, note, has a specially Judaic basis, our main legend is connected with that greatest Jewish law giver and ruler, Solomon. Our present doctrine is a Trinitarianism, clothed with the Christian virtues. If Freemasonry arose as an entirely new scheme in the 16th or 17th century it must have arisen in a Christian land, and would certainly have been marked by specially Trinitarian features, which would have remained permanent.

Now as collateral evidence of my contention I pray you to follow me into the consideration that in our Freemasonry may yet be traced allusions and references to that system of esoteric teaching and dogma, which was undeniably the result of the destruction of the exoteric Monotheism of Judea, I mean the Jewish Kabbalah which first took shape as a definite secret Sophia, wisdom or doctrine after the Fall of Jerusalem, and which was founded on the basis of the Monotheistic truths accumulated during centuries of more or less pure outward observance of a Monotheistic religion.

This Kabbalah then crystallized gradually into a theological scheme, and became more and more elaborated through the dark-ages following the ruin of the Augustan era; to dominant paganism followed utter ignorance of the masses until a dawn arose in Europe and a Monotheism was developed anew, not Jewish, but Christian, and became exoteric, and its exotericism became its weakness, and its priesthood became once more self-seeking, and neglected the primal truth-yet even through this period the esoteric purity was preserved by the few, by the learned, by the pious.

I will not wander into the area of discussion which rages around the sole origin of Freemasonry from trade guilds, from Templarism, from the Jewish race, from the Hermeticists, or from the Rosicrucians.

I am content to recognize that all these associations have been concerned in its growth, and am content that our present system points only to the cardinal truth, confessing that in its progression along the ladder of time it has been assisted by each and all of these, and has survived them, and has thus proved its right to exist. To say the least of it, the mystery would only be increased by a dogma that the officials of Freemasonry in the seventeenth century were so intensely learned that they constructed proprio motu, such a system, in which the doctrines and essays of the most ancient Aporreta shine forth.

The Kabbalah as a system of Theosophy has pre-eminent claims to be considered *primus inter pares*, among all the theistic speculations of mankind, which have a bearing on, and have taken part in the formation of, the Masonic Aphanism. I shall briefly point out a few masonic points which are illuminated by a comparison with the Kabbalah. Some references to the mysteries are conveniently interspersed, of these there is much evidence that the Egyptian forms are the oldest; now it must be specially remembered that the Lecture on the Tracing Board of the first degree actually refers to these customs of the ancient Egyptians as the fount of origin for many masonic points; it refers also to the doctrines of Pythagoras whose five pointed star I mention later on.

Among the masonic points, which have been derived from the ancient mysteries, I notice the triple degrees of the system, corresponding to the mysteries of Serapis, Iris, and Osiris. Now our second degree has feminine suggestions; note, Shibboleth, the ear of corn, the water, for corn refers to the goddess Ceres, female, or Demeter, Gemeter, earth mother, and water is female in all old languages; compare Binah, mother deity; and our third is a very close approximation to that which represented the slaying of Osiris. The battery of acclamation when the candidate is restored to light is a direct imitation of the sudden clash of feigned thunder and lightning by which the neophyte of the Eleusinian mysteries was greeted. The death of Osiris and resurrection as Horus are represented as the decease of the fellow craft and the raising of a new master mason.

The entered apprentice is referred to three lights, these are Osiris in the east, Isis in the west, and Horus who was master or living lord in place of Osiris, in the south. Note also that there is no light in the north, the type of night and of darkness, in this also the idea is an ancient one. The three great, though emblematic lights compose a bright triangle, the three lesser lights an inferior or darker one, the two combined may be considered in a group as a six-pointed star, the Hexapla, or Seal of Solomon, which was also a notable emblem in all the old initiations. The Hexapla was a type of the number six, esteemed a male number assigned by the Kabbalists to Microprosopus, the *Vau* of the Hebrew alphabet, and of the Tetragrammaton, the six middle Sephiroth, especially the median 6th, the Tiphereth, or Beauty of the Deity.

The Pentalpha, or emblem of health, the Pythagorean emblem, is the five-pointed Masonic star, five in the Hebrew *He*, a female potency according to the Kabbalah, and may be either the superior *He*, the mother idea, or the lower *He*, the Bride of God, the Church. The Kingdom, the two together constitute the Elohim, a feminine plural noun, constantly used as a title for creative power in the narrative of Genesis in chapter one, and up to the end of verse four of chapter two, where the Jehovist narrative commences.

It is a curious coincidence that the Acacia referring to the burial of Hiram Abiff, and which the fellowcrafts, dressed in white, carried in their hands as emblems of their innocence, is the same word as the Greek ἀκακία, which means innocence; it was also an emblem of mortality.

The insistence on a candidate for masonry proving himself free from deformity is a requirement which was common to the selection from among the Levites of a priest of the Jews (see Leviticus xxi., 18), and to the reception of a neophyte in both the Egyptian and the Eleusinian mysteries, and a further point of resemblance is seen in the refusal to admit a slave, or any but a free man. If the whole aim of Freemasonry were to propagate brotherly love and charity, why refuse to extend its blessings to the cripple, or the maimed, or to him in subjection.

The legend of the Three Grand Masters, of whom one is lost—becomes removed to the invisible world—is a curious image of the Kabbalistic first triad of the emanations of the unseen and unknowable Ain Soph Aur, the boundless one, boundless light, first is Kether the Crown, thence proceed Chochmah and Binah, wisdom and understanding, and then is the Crown concealed and lost to perception in its exaltedness, the word is lost and replaced by other titles.

In the Ten Sephiroth, as in our Lodges, we are taught of two great pillars, one on the right and on the left, the pillars of Mercy and Judgment; then a third exists between them, that of severity, tempered by mercy, and called pillar of Mildness. These are similar to the Masonic pillars of Wisdom, Strength and Beauty, while the Ain Soph Aur above them is the Mystic Blazing Star in the East. Wisdom Strength and Beauty are the Sephirotic Triad of Chochmah, Geburah, and Tiphereth.

The several emanations of the Sephiroth of the Kabbalah, one proceeding from the other, produce, as they are always designed in visible form, a tortuous path, at once reminding us of the Winding Staircase. Indeed one form of the contemplation of the Eternal was described by the Kabbalists as ascending by the Sephirotic names and descending by the paths. This tortuous path is also like the lightning flash, as is said in the "Sepher Yetzirah" or "Book of Formations," which has been translated by myself, and is, perhaps, the oldest monotheistic philosophical tract in existence. Note, the Son of God is also spoken of as the "Light of the World."

Four tassels refer to four cardinal virtues, says the first

degree Tracing Board Lecture, these are temperance, fortitude, prudence, and justice; these again were originally branches of the Sephirotic Tree, Chesed first, Netzah fortitude, Binah prudence, and Geburah justice. Virtue, honor, and mercy, another triad, are Chochmah, Hod, and Chesed.

Another well-known Sephiroth Triad deserves mention here, the concluding phrase of the Lord's Prayer, of the Prayer Book version, which, however, is not found in the Douay version, nor in the revised New Testament, viz: the kingdom, the power, and the glory—Malkuth, Netzah, and Hod.

As may be seen by the diagram many triads may be formed, and different authors speak of different numbers; thus Frater S. C. Gould, of Manchester, New Hampshire, describes nine; Fra. MacGregor Mathers notes ten but even more may be formed, of course, if relative sequence be not insisted upon.

The Winding Staircase consisted of 3, 5 and 7 steps, if not of more, of these, three referred to the three Rulers of a Lodge, these are the three mother letters of the Hebrew alphabet, *Aleph, Mem, Shin,* typical again of fire, air, and water, the three first Sephiroth. Five to hold a Lodge and seven to make it perfect, these are the Hebrew seven double letters, parallel emblems to seven planets and seven lower Sephiroth. Three, five and seven amount to fifteen, which is equivalent to JAH, God, *Yod,* and *He,* ten and five; every Hebrew word is also a number, and the reverse. These seven persons, again, are typical of the seven most learned Rabbis who held the Assembly named in the Zohar, Idra Suta, in which the essence of Deity is discussed as a Holy Mystery. The still more Holy Assembly of Rabbis, the Idra Rabba included three more, these formed the Keepers of the Veils of the original Royal Arch Chapter, for whom the lower offices of Treasurer, Inner Guard and Sentinel are now substituted; some very learned patron of the order caused this change to be made, fearing that it might be a blasphemy to represent these three highest powers in a Lodge which might become too ordinary a business. They were types of the first Sephirotic Triad. Freemasons little know how close they have been to the personation of the most exalted types of Omnipotence.

The letter G in the center of a Fellowcrafts' Lodge, has received several explanations; I would add that it has a relation to *Gimel*, the Hebrew G, the third letter of the alphabet, the three, meaning Trinity of Deity; the third Sephira is Binah, the mother of Microprosopus, the son, a feminine potency, Mother of God, with uncial Greek capital G. The present masonic interpretation is folly, the idea of a modern ornamental lecturer.

Again the two parallel lines, the one Moses, the other King Solomon, enclosing a circle, bearing a central point, is entirely Kabbalistic. The point is Tiphereth, beauty of conduct within a circle of virtues and bounded by the pillars Mercy and Justice.

Regard for a moment the varying titles; Great Architect, the Foundation, Yesod the center of the lowest triad.

Grand Geometrician, the beauty of design, Tiphereth, center of the median triad.

Most High, the awful Kether, the Crown, partly concealed, at sight of whose face a mortal, unprepared, must die. Notice the grandeur and mystery increases as we pass up the Masonic ladder or the Sephirotic Tree.

The perambulation by the candidate under appropriate

guidance is an apt imitation of the ceremony in the Ancient Mysteries.

Another remnant of the same form was until recently, and may be still, extant in Scotland, the highland custom Deasil was to walk three times round a person in the direction of the sun, for favorable effect. To perambulate against the sun was called Widdershins, and was an evil omen and act.

Freemasonry, as one special development of a long series of Monotheistic secret associations, being constituted on a basis of masonic operations by masculine operatives, has perhaps necessarily excluded females; many military and hierarchical mystical societies have also from their essence consisted of males alone. The very low state of female culture in the ancient world and during the middle ages, also no doubt contributed towards the exclusion of women from mystic rites and from active interference with religions ceremonies; an exclusion which, were we about to constitute a new form of concealed worship, would hardly be tolerated in the present year of grace, and certainly could not be defended in argument. This ancient exclusion of women from secret rites (*to which there were a few exceptions*) has been expanded also in another direction, with baneful result: I refer to the complete removal of all female types, forms, and stages from the ideas of the higher powers, angels, archangels, and the emanations of Deity, which certainly existed in the oldest forms of the Kabbalah, and in the minds of the composers of the early chapters of the Pentateuch. It cannot be doubted that a very large number of minds cling firmly to the Roman Catholic type of religion, owing to its insistence of reverence and praise to the beatified woman—Mary—who is representative of the ancient views of the female counterpart of God-head.

With this digression I must conclude, and I beg for a lenient judgment on these discursive remarks on our mystic order, for even if the views be erroneous, they may yet call up a refutation which shall be found of great value to the brethren present, and Freemasons in general.

Spiritual Progress

by Helena P. Blavatsky

Christian Rossetti's well-known lines:

Does the road wind up-hill all the way?
Yes, to the very end.
Will the day's journey take the whole long day?
From morn to night, my friend.

are like an epitome of the life of those who are truly treading the path which leads to higher things. Whatever differences are to be found in the various presentations of the Esoteric Doctrine, as in every age it donned a fresh garment, different both in hue and texture to that which preceded, yet in every one of them we find the fullest agreement upon one point -- the road to spiritual development. One only inflexible rule has been ever binding upon the neophyte, as it is binding now -- the *complete* subjugation of the lower nature by the higher. From the Vedas and Upanishads to the recently published *Light on the Path,* search as we may through the bibles of every race and cult, we find but one only way, -- hard, painful, troublesome, by which man can gain the true spiritual insight. And how can it be otherwise since all religions and all philosophies are but the variants of the first teachings of the One Wisdom, imparted to men at the beginning of the cycle by the Planetary Spirit? The true Adept, the developed man, must, we are always told, *become* -- he cannot be made. The process is therefore one of growth through evolution, and this must necessarily involve a certain amount of pain. The main cause of pain lies in our perpetually seeking the permanent in the impermanent, and not only seeking, but acting as if we had already found the unchangeable, in a world of which the one certain quality we can predicate is constant change, and always, just as we fancy we have taken a firm hold upon the permanent, it changes within our very grasp, and pain results. Again, the idea of growth involves also the idea of disruption, the inner being must continually burst through its confining shell or encasement, and such a disruption must also be accompanied by pain, not physical but mental and intellectual. And this is how it is, in the course of our lives, the trouble that comes upon us is always just the one we feel to be the hardest that could possibly happen -- it is always the one thing we feel we cannot possibly bear. If we look at it from a wider point of view, we shall see that we are trying to burst through our shell at its one vulnerable point; that our growth, to be real growth, and not the collective result of a series of excrescences, must progress evenly throughout, just as the body of a child grows, not first the head and then a hand, followed perhaps by a leg; but in all directions at once, regularly and imperceptibly. Man's tendency is to cultivate each part separately, neglecting the others in the meantime -- every crushing pain is caused by the expansion of some neglected part, which expansion is rendered more difficult by the effects of the cultivation bestowed elsewhere. Evil is often the result of over-anxiety, and men are always trying to do too much, they are not content to leave well alone, to do always just what the occasion demands and no more, they exaggerate every action and so produce karma to be worked out in a future birth. One of the subtlest forms of this evil is the hope and desire of reward. Many there are who, albeit often unconsciously, are yet spoiling all their efforts by entertaining this idea of reward, and allowing it to become an active factor in their lives and so leaving the door open to anxiety, doubt, fear, despondency -- failure. The goal of the aspirant for spiritual wisdom, is entrance upon a higher plane of existence; he is to become a new man, more perfect in every way than he is at present, and if he succeeds, his capabilities and faculties will receive a corresponding increase of range and power, just as in the visible world we find that each stage in the evolutionary scale is marked by increase of capacity. This is how it is that the Adept becomes endowed with marvelous powers that have been so often described, but the main point to be remembered is, that these powers are the natural accompaniments of existence on a higher plane of evolution, just as the ordinary human faculties are the natural accompaniments of existence on the ordinary human plane.

Many persons seem to think that adeptship is not so much the result of radical development as of additional construction; they seem to imagine that an Adept is a man, who, by going through a certain plainly defined course of training, consisting of minute attention to a set of arbitrary rules, acquires first one power and then another and when he has attained a certain number of these powers is forthwith dubbed an adept. Acting on this mistaken idea they fancy that the first thing to be done towards attaining adeptship is to acquire "powers" -- clairvoyance and the power of leaving the physical body and travelling to a distance, are among those which fascinate the most. To those who wish to acquire such powers for their own private advantage, we have nothing to say, they fall under the condemnation of all who act for purely selfish ends. But there are others, who, mistaking effect for cause, honestly think that the acquirement of abnormal powers is the only road to spiritual advancement. These look upon our Society as merely the readiest means to enable them to gain knowledge in this direction, considering it as a sort of occult academy, an institution established to afford facilities for the instruction of would-be miracle-workers. In spite of repeated protests and warnings, there are some minds in whom this notion seems ineradicably fixed, and they are loud in their expressions of disappointment when they find that what had been previously told them is perfectly true; that the Society was founded to teach no new and easy paths to the acquisition of "powers"; and that its only mission is to re-kindle the torch of truth, so long extinguished for all but the very few, and to keep that truth alive by the formation of a fraternal union of mankind, the only soil in which the good seed can grow. The Theosophical Society does indeed desire to promote the spiritual growth of every individual who comes within its influence, but its methods are those of the ancient Rishis, its tenets those of the oldest Esotericism; it is no dispenser of patent nostrums composed of violent remedies which no honest healer would dare to use. It appears that various societies have sprung into existence since the foundation of the Theosophical Society, profiting by the interest the latter has awakened in matters of psychic research, and endeavoring to gain members by promising them easy acquirement of psychic powers. In India we have long been familiar with the existence of hosts of sham ascetics of all descriptions, and we fear that there is fresh danger in this direction, here, as well as in Europe and America. In this connection we would warn all our members, and others who are seeking spiritual knowledge, to beware of persons offering to teach them easy methods of acquiring psychic gifts, such gifts are indeed comparatively easy of acquirement by artificial means, but fade out as soon as the nerve-stimulus exhausts itself. The real seership and adeptship which is accompanied by true psychic development, once reached is never lost.

The Treasure of Treasures for Alchemists

by Paracelsus

Part I

Nature begets a mineral in the bowels of the earth. There are two kinds of it, which are found in many districts of Europe. The best which has been offered to me, which also has been found genuine in experimentation, is externally in the figure of the greater world, and is in the eastern part of the sphere of the Sun. The other, in the Southern Star, is now in its first efflorescence. The bowels of the earth thrust this forth through its surface. It is found red in its first coagulation, and in it lie hid all the flowers and colors of the minerals. Much has been written about it by the philosophers, for it is of a cold and moist nature, and agrees with the element of water.

So far as relates to the knowledge of it and experiment with it, all the philosophers before me, though they have aimed at it with their missiles, have gone very wide of the mark. They believed that Mercury and Sulphur were the mother of all metals, never even dreaming of making mention meanwhile of a third; and yet when the water is separated from it by Spagyric Art the truth is plainly revealed, though it was unknown to Galen or to Avicenna. But if, for the sake of our excellent physicians, we had to describe only the name, the composition; the dissolution, and coagulation, as in the beginning of the world Nature proceeds with all growing things, a whole year would scarcely suffice me, and, in order to explain these things, not even the skins of numerous cows would be adequate.

Now, I assert that in this mineral are found three

principles, which are Mercury, Sulphur, and the Mineral Water which has served to naturally coagulate it. Spagyric science is able to extract this last from its proper juice when it is not altogether matured, in the middle of the autumn, just like a pear from a tree. The tree potentially contains the pear. If the Celestial Stars and Nature agree, the tree first of all puts forth shoots in the month of March; then it thrusts out buds, and when these open the flower appears, and so on in due order until in autumn the pear grows ripe. So is it with the minerals. These are born, in like manner, in the bowels of the earth. Let the Alchemists who are seeking the Treasure of Treasures carefully note this. I will show them the way, its beginning, its middle, and its end. In the following treatise I will describe the proper Water, the proper Sulphur, and the proper Balm thereof. By means of these three the resolution and composition are coagulated into one.

The Treasure of Treasures for Alchemists

Part II

Concerning the Sulphur of Cinnabar

Take mineral Cinnabar and prepare it in the following manner. Cook it with rain water in a stone vessel for three hours. Then purify it carefully, and dissolve it in Aqua Regis, which is composed of equal parts of vitriol, nitre, and sal ammoniac. Another formula is vitriol, saltpeter, alum, and common salt.

Distil this in an alembic. Pour it on again, and separate carefully the pure from the impure thus. Let it putrefy for a month in horse-dung; then separate the elements in the following manner. If it puts forth its sign, commence the distillation by means of an alembic with a fire of the first degree. The water and the air will ascend; the fire and the earth will remain at the bottom. Afterwards join them again, and gradually treat with the ashes. So the water and the air will again ascend first, and afterwards the element of fire, which expert artists recognize. The earth will remain in the bottom of the vessel. This collect there. It is what many seek after and few find.

This dead earth in the reverberatory you will prepare according to the rules of Art, and afterwards add fire of the first degree for five days and nights. When these have elapsed you must apply the second degree for the same number of days and nights, and proceed according to Art with the material enclosed. At length you will find a volatile salt, like a thin alkali, containing in itself the Astrum of fire and earth. Mix this with the two elements that have been preserved, the water and the earth. Again place it on the ashes for eight days and eight nights, and you will find that which has been neglected by many Artists. Separate this according to your experience, and according to the rules of the Spagyric Art, and you will have a white earth, from which its color has been extracted. Join the element of fire and salt to the alkalized earth. Digest in a pelican to extract the essence. Then a new earth will be deposited, which put aside.

The Treasure of Treasures for Alchemists

Part III

Concerning the Red Lion

Afterwards take the lion in the pelican which also is found at first, when you see its tincture, that is to say, the element of fire which stands above the water, the air, and the earth. Separate it from its deposit by trituration. Thus you will have the true aurum potabile. Sweeten this with the alcohol of wine poured over it, and then distil in an alembic until you perceive no acidity to remain in the Aqua Regia.

This Oil of the Sun, enclosed in a retort hermetically sealed, you must place for elevation that it may be exalted and doubled in its degree. Then put the vessel, still closely shut, in a cool place. Thus it will not be dissolved, but coagulated. Place it again for elevation and coagulation, and repeat this three times. Thus will be produced the Tincture of the Sun, perfect in its degree. Keep this in its own place.

The Treasure of Treasures for Alchemists

Part IV

Concerning the Green Lion

Take the vitriol of Venus, carefully prepared according to the rules of Spagyric Art; and add thereto the elements of water and air which you have reserved. Resolve, and set to putrefy for a month according to instructions. When the putrefaction is finished, you will behold the sign of the elements. Separate, and you will soon see two colors, namely, white and red. The red is above the white. The red tincture of the vitriol is so powerful that it reddens all white bodies, and whitens all red ones, which is wonderful.

Work upon this tincture by means of a retort, and you will perceive a blackness issue forth. Treat it again by means of the retort, repeating the operation until it comes out whitish. Go on, and do not despair of the work. Rectify until you find the true, clear Green Lion, which you will recognize by its great weight. You will see that it is heavy and large. This is the Tincture, transparent gold. You will see marvelous signs of this Green Lion, such as could be bought by no treasures of the Roman Leo. Happy he who has learnt how to find it and use it for a tincture!

This is the true and genuine Balsam, the Balsam of the Heavenly Stars, suffering no bodies to decay, nor allowing leprosy, gout, or dropsy to take root. It is given in a dose of one grain, if it has been fermented with Sulphur of Gold.

Ah, Charles the German, where is your treasure? Where

are your philosophers? Where your doctors? Where are your decocters of woods, who at least purge and relax? Is your heaven reversed? Have your stars wandered out of their course, and are they straying in another orbit, away from the line of limitation, since your eyes are smitten with blindness, as by a carbuncle, and other things making a show of ornament, beauty, and pomp? If your artists only knew that their prince Galen - they call none like him - was sticking in hell, from whence he has sent letters to me, they would make the sign of the cross upon themselves with a fox's tail. In the same way your Avicenna sits in the vestibule of the infernal portal; and I have disputed with him about his aurum potabile, his Tincture of the Philosophers, his Quintessence, and Philosophers' Stone, his Mithridatic, his Theriac, and all the rest. O, you hypocrites, who despise the truths taught you by a true physician, who is himself instructed by Nature, and is a son of God himself! Come, then, and listen, impostors who prevail only by the authority of your high positions! After my death, my disciples will burst forth and drag you to the light, and shall expose your dirty drugs, wherewith up to this time you have compassed the death of princes, and the most invincible magnates of the Christian world. Woe for your necks in the day of judgment! I know that the monarchy will be mine. Mine, too, will be the honor and glory. Not that I praise myself: Nature praises me. Of her I am born; her I follow. She knows me, and I know her. The light which is in her I have beheld in her; outside, too, I have proved the same in the figure of the microcosm, and found it in that universe.

But I must proceed with my design in order to satisfy my disciples to the full extent of their wish. I willingly do this for them, if only skilled in the light of Nature and thoroughly practiced in astral matters, they finally become adepts in philosophy, which enables them to know the nature of every kind of water.

Take, then, of this liquid of the minerals which I have described, four parts by weight of the Earth, of red Sol two parts, of Sulphur of Sol one part. Put these together into a pelican, congelate, and dissolve them three times. Thus you will have the Tincture of the Alchemists. We have not here described its weight: but this is given in the book on Transmutations.

So, now, he who has one to a thousand ounces of the Astrum Solis shall also tinge his own body of Sol.

If you have the Astrum of Mercury, in the same manner, you will tinge the whole body of common Mercury. If you have the Astrum of Venus you will, in like manner, tinge the whole body of Venus, and change it into the best metal. These facts have all been proved. The same must also be understood as to the Astra of the other planets, as Saturn, Jupiter, Mars, Luna, and the rest. For tinctures are also prepared from these: concerning which we now make no mention in this place, because we have already dwelt at sufficient length upon them in the book on the Nature of Things and in the Archidoxies. So, too, the first entity of metals and terrestrial minerals have been made, sufficiently clear for Alchemists to enable them to get the Alchemists' Tincture.

This work, the Tincture of the Alchemists, need not be one of nine months; but quickly, and without any delay, you may go on by the Spaygric Art of the Alchemists, and, in the space of forty days, you can fix this alchemical substance, exalt it, putrefy it, ferment it, coagulate it into a stone, and produce the Alchemical Phoenix. But it should be noted well that the Sulphur of Cinnabar becomes the Flying Eagle, whose wings fly away without wind, and carry the body of the phoenix to the nest of the parent, where it is nourished by the element of fire, and the young ones dig out its eyes: from whence there emerges a whiteness, divided in its sphere, into a sphere and life out of its own heart, by the balsam of its inward parts, according to the property of the cabalists.

Instructions on Crystal Gazing

by L. W. de Laurence

It will have been noticed by the student that the ancient methods of Crystal-Gazing for purposes of "divination" involved a somewhat elaborate ritual, including the use of swords, pentacles, candles, and many of the accompaniments usual to the performance of Magical rites, in by-gone ages, when the object in view was not as at present, the cultivation of mere "Personal Clairvoyance" in the gazer, but rather to compel the actual presence in the Crystal of certain genii or spirits, and to obtain therefrom answers to such questions as might be propounded by the querent.

While, therefore, it has been of interest to write in the foregoing pages the historical aspect of this subject, it will be well for all persons into whose hands this book may fall to remember carefully the two following points:

(**a**) That the modus operandi pursued by certain of the ancients, and in which the paraphernalia and ritual described were utilized, was one involving dangers of no mean order, as has been already pointed out, and could only be properly made use of by highly qualified votaries who had received personal training under some practical Adept and Master of the ceremonial, who understood the unseen forces of the spiritual world, both good and evil, and the necessary steps to be taken for protecting themselves from possible injury, or even death, through the medium of wicked intelligences.

(**b**) That as the ordinary experimenter of today has

no desire to compel the presence of a spiritual being in the Crystal, it is quite unnecessary for him or her to draw magic circles, or to go to the trouble and expense of acquiring and using special or costly apparatus, with the exception of the Crystal itself.

What is desired is through the regular use of the Gazing Crystal to cultivate a personal degree of Clairvoyant power, so that visions of things or events, past, present, and future, may appear clearly to the interior vision, or eye of the soul.

In the pursuit of this effort only, the Crystal becomes at once both a valuable, interesting, and useful channel of development and instruction, shorn of its former dangers, and rendered conducive to spiritual development.

To the attainment of this desirable end, attention is asked to the following practical directions, which, if carefully followed, will lead to success:

First. Select a quiet room where you will be entirely undisturbed, taking care that it is as far as possible free from mirrors, ornaments, pictures, glaring colors, and the like, which may otherwise distract the attention.

The room should be of comfortable temperature in accordance with the time of year, neither hot or cold. About 60° to 65° F is suitable in most cases, though allowance can be made where necessary for natural differences in the temperaments of various persons. Thus thin, nervous, delicately-organized individuals, and those of lymphatic and soft, easy-going, passive types, require a slightly warmer apartment than the more positive class, who are known by their dark eyes, hair, and complexion, combined with more prominent joints and sharper development of what phrenologists term the Perceptive region of the forehead. Should a fire, or any form of artificial light be necessary, it should be well screened off, so as to prevent the light rays from being reflected in, or in any manner directly reaching the Crystal.

The room should not be dark, but rather shadowed, or charged with a dull light, somewhat such as prevails on a cloudy or wet day.

Second. The Crystal should be placed on its stand on a table, or it may rest on a black velvet cushion, but in either case it should be partially surrounded by a black silk or similar wrap or screen, so adjusted as to cut off any undesirable reflection.

Before beginning to experiment, remember that most frequently nothing will be seen on the first occasion, and possibly not for several settings, though some sitters, if strongly gifted with physic powers in a state of unconscious, and sometimes conscious degree of unfoldment, may be fortunate enough to obtain good results at the very first trial, especially if a small amount of Temple Intense is burned just before using the Crystal.

If, therefore, nothing is perceived during the first few attempts, do not despair or become impatient, or imagine that you will never see anything.

There is a royal road to Crystal vision, but it is open only to the compound password of Calmness, Patience, and Perseverance. If at the first attempt to playing a piano or riding a bicycle failure ensues, the only way to learn is to pay attention to the necessary rules, and to persevere daily until the ability to play or ride comes naturally.

Thus it is with the would-be seer. Persevere in accordance with these simple directions, and success will sooner or later crown your efforts.

Third. Commence by sitting comfortably with the eyes fixed upon the Crystal, not by a fierce stare, but with a steady, calm gaze, for thirty minutes only, on the first occasion. In taking the time it is best to stand your clock at a distance, where, while the face is clearly visible, the ticking is rendered almost inaudible. When the time is up, carefully put the Crystal away in its case, and keep it in a dark place, under lock and key, allowing no one but yourself to handle it.

At the second sitting, which should be at the same place in the same position, and at the same time, you may increase the length of the effort to forty minutes, and continue for this period during the next five or six sittings, after which the time may be gradually increased, but should in no case exceed two hours. This precise order of repetition is always to be followed until the disciple has developed an almost automatic ability to readily obtain results, when it need no longer be adhered to.

Fourth. Any person or persons admitted to the room, and allowed to remain while you sit, should-

(a) keep absolute silence, and
(b) remain seated at a distance from you.

When you have developed your Occult powers, questions may, of course, be put to you by one of those present, but even then only in a very gentle, or low and slow tone of voice; never suddenly, or in a forceful manner.

Fifth. When you find the Crystal begins to look dull or cloudy, with small pin points of light glittering therein, like tiny stars, you may know that you are commencing to obtain that for which you seek — viz., "Crystalline vision." Therefore persevere with confidence. This condition may, or may not, continue for several sittings, the Crystal seeming at times to alternately appear and disappear, as in a mist. By and by this hazy appearance will in its turn give place quite suddenly to a blindness of the senses to all else but a blue or bluish ocean of space, against which, as if it were a background, the vision will be clearly apparent.

Sixth. The Crystal should not be used soon after taking a meal, and care should be taken in matters of diet to partake only of digestible foods, and to avoid alcoholic beverages. Plain and nourishing food, and outdoor exercise, with contentment of mind, or love of simplicity in living, are great aids to success. Mental anxiety, or ill-health, are not conducive to the desired end. Attention to correct breathing is of importance.

Seventh. As regards the time at which events seen will come to pass, each Crystal-Gazer is usually impressed with regard thereto; but, as a general rule, visions appearing in the extreme background indicate time more remote, either past or future, than those perceived nearer at hand, while those appearing in the forefront, or close to the seer, denote the present, or immediate future.

Eighth. Two principal classes of visions will present themselves to the sitter —

(**a**) The Symbolic, indicated by the appearance of symbols such as a flag, boat, knife, gold, etc.; and (**b**) Actual Scenes and Personages, in action or otherwise.

Persons of a Positive cast of organization, the more active, excitable, yet decided type, are most likely to perceive symbolically, or allegorically; while those of a Passive nature usually receive direct or literal revelations. Both classes will find it necessary to carefully cultivate truthfulness, unselfishness, gratitude for what is shown, and absolute confidence in their own ability to concentrate the mind.

Mystical Realization

by Arthur Edward Waite

The testimony to mystical experience has been borne in the modem world, in the main on the faith of the records, and under the Christian aegis - through all the Christian centuries- it has been borne at first hand by those who have attained therein some part at least of that which awaits the souls of men in the fruition of Divine Union. The annals of old sanctity and the commentaries of expert theology constitute together an exceedingly large literature, over and above which there is a yet larger testimony going back into remote ages and concerned with the same experience under the denominations of other religions in the sacred world of the East. Yet it seems to me that in what has been called the "general and popular world" of thoughtful and literate people there is still only a very slight and imperfect understanding of the whole subject. There is, I think, none on which statements, are looser and fundamental misconceptions, more frequent. The terms Mysticism and Mystical are still used to characterize the dealings of "occult science" and as synonyms for the scheme of things, which are usually connoted by the title of "new thought." They are labels in common, used indifferently by friends and enemies of both. Those who affirm that there are no occult sciences, though there are many grades of self-induced hallucination, are apt to term them mystical as a by-word of reproach. Those in whose view the literary ventures which carry the mark of new thought are goods that are labeled falsely, regard it as the last word of condemnation to describe them as mystical. On the other hand, both literatures belong, in the opinion of many defenders, to the realm of mysticism, which they understand to mean higher thought. The point of union between the two parties resides in the fact that they are indifferently misusing words.

It happens that mysticism is the world-old science of the soul's return to God and that those who apply it to (1) any form of conventional metaphysics, (2) any branch of mental philosophy, (3) any reveries high or low, are no less mistaken than those who use it as a term of scorn. I care nothing in this connection for the etymological significance of the word, as denoting what is secret and withdrawn. It has come in the course of the years to have one meaning only in the accurate use thereof, and we must abide by this and no other-for the sake of ordered thought-unless and until the keepers of mystical science shall agree between themselves on another and more definite term as an expression of the whole subject.

I have been speaking of the outer circles, from whom it seems idle at present to expect accuracy; but there is a more extraordinary want of understanding on the part of some whom we should expect to be capable at least of thinking rightly within the elementary measures of mysticism. Here it is no longer a question concerning the mere word, or the use of denominations in the sense of the mystical path when they belong more properly to the end, after all the travelings are over. I refer especially at the moment to misapprehensions respecting the place of the science in the life of modern man and woman, and this involves a consideration of the now recurring question whether that science can be acquired by practice in the daily life of the world. There can be no expectation of presenting in a brief space any views that will differ materially from those which I have expressed already in much longer studies; but it may be possible to offer something simply, for understanding on the part of those who cannot examine the subject in ordered and lengthy books. The question is, therefore, whether those excellent people are right who seem to think that the principles of mystical science may be so put forward that they can be taken into the heart, not indeed of the men in the street -though no one wishes to exclude them-but of men and women everywhere who have turned already to God, or are disposed in that direction. Alternatively, is it-shall I say ?-a science which is reserved to experts only? We know that it is not possible to become acquainted readily and easily with the higher mathematics, with chemistry or biology. There are certain natural qualifications in virtue of which the poet is born, as well as made subsequently; there is also the scientific mind, which presupposes gift and faculty, as well as opportunity and application. In the science of the mystics, in their peculiar art of life, are there certain essential qualifications to be postulated in every case, and is there a long apprenticeship? Before attempting to answer, let us see what is being said and how far it exhibits any adequate acquaintance with the problems belonging to the debate.

It has been suggested recently that religion is at work revising institutions and theology, that reconstruction is in the air everywhere and that mysticism needs reconstruction as much as anything else. In the face of this statement a certain caution is necessary lest we begin to talk foolishly. It appears, however, that the remark applies rather to notions, theories and systems, to "the spell of medieval mysticism" and to the reconstruction of these. Yet the tendency is to regard mysticism as a mode of thought, an attitude -if you like- towards the universal, so that we can have done with archaic forms and devise others which are modem. It is, however, as I have said, a science, the end of which is attained in the following of certain methods. One does not change sciences -as, for example, mathematics- but we can reconstruct and, it may be, improve our way of acquiring them. Medieval mysticism is the same as modern mysticism, but there may be other ways of reaching it, in respect of the externals, than were known and practiced in convents. Fundamentally speaking, however, the ways are one- whether in the East or West, for those who follow *Vedanta* and those to whom the *Imitation* is a source. The only change that we can make is by taking out of the way that which is unnecessary thereto. As I tried to show some four or five years since, in *The Way Of Divine Union,* there is no question that the end of mysticism was reached by the ascetic path during many past centuries of Christendom, but it belonged to the accidents of the quest; and other ways are possible, which I tried also to indicate. The alleged reconstruction of religion is taking place only in a subsidiary sense, within narrow measures, or here and there in the corners. The great Latin Church is revising nothing, while the Greek -I suppose- is stewing in the waters of its own incapacity. But if they were both at the work of remaking and at one in their activity with the sects and the Anglican Church, the case of the mystics would still differ, because pure mysticism has no institutions to revise and no conventional or official theology to expand, reduce, or vary. It is a path of advancement towards a certain end, and the path is one: the variations are found only in the modes of travelling. Having in this manner cleared the issues, there must be something said of the end and the way thereto.

There is a great experiment possible in this life and there is a great crown of the experiment, but in the nature of things it is not to be bought cheaply, for it demands the whole man. It has been said that the life of the mystic is one of awareness of God, and as to this we must remember that we are dealing with a question of life and a life-problem. But what is awareness of God? It is a certain inward realization, a consciousness of His Divine -not only without us but within. The word awareness is therefore good and true, but it is one of those intimations which -as I have suggested already- are of the path and not of the end. It is of the learner and not of the scientist. The proof can be put in a nutshell by an appeal to the perfect analogy of that experience which is human love. Can we say to the human over that an awareness of the beloved must content him here and now? But that which he seeks is possession, after the manner of all in all- possession which is reciprocal and mutual. In Divine Things the word is realization, and mystical realization is the state of being possessed and possessing. Otherwise, it is God in us and we in God: O' state of the ineffable, beyond all words and thoughts, deeper than tears of the heart and higher than all its raptures. The science of the mystic is that of the peculiar life-cultus, life-practice, or quest of life which leads to this state. In respect both of path and state the word is love. That kind of loving is summarized in the grand old counsel: "With all thy heart and with all thy soul." The rewards of love are not those which can be earned by divided allegiance. There is also another saying -about the desire of a certain house having eaten one up. There is no eye on two worlds in this and no Sabbath dedication except in the long Sabbath of undivided life. Here, too, is no art of making the best of both worlds and especially of this one, as if with one eye on the dollars and another on God. In this kind of dedication the world goes by and the pageants of all its temples: there are no half-measures respecting it. The motto of the path is *sub specie adernitatis,* and it connotes the awakening and subsequent activity of a particular inward faculty. We know well enough by experience the power of a ruling passion, and it may happen to be one that is lawful. The man who is ruled thereby is living *sub specie ilia;* it colors all his ways and days: it is the very motive of his life. Now, if we postulate in certain persons a ruling passion for God, it is then *sub ilia specie* that they live and move and have their being.

As regards this state and as regards its gifts and fruits, even at the early stages, I testify that the Divine in the universe answers to the Divine in man. There does take place that which maintains and feeds the passion. A life which is turned to the keynote of the eternal mode knows of the things that are eternal. It knows very soon that it is not on a false quest: that God is and that He recompenses those who seek Him out is verified by valid experience. It grows from more to more, an ever-expanding equipment in Lightest sanity of mind. Two things are certain: (1) apart from this high passion there can be no practical mystic; but (2) no one can teach another how to acquire it. Once it has been kindled in the heart, the secret of the path is its maintenance, and many devices have been tried- among others those of the ascetics. The only excellent way is that of love in its activity towards all in God and God in all. This is the sense of St. Augustine's Love and do what you will. Hatred is a canker in the heart and eats up this passion. Universal love maintains the passion for God till that time when God enters and takes over the work; it is then the beginning of the end, and that end is the still activity of union in the Eternal Centre. It is inevitable that vocation must be postulated, but this signifies an inward possibility of response to an ever-recurring call. It is thus that the divine passion is kindled which -as I have said- no one can communicate to another. There is something in the individual fount by which some are poets and some are called to the priesthood. For the same inscrutable reason there are some who receive and answer the call to mystic life. It may be a consequence of antecedent lives or of hidden leading from spiritual spheres: I do not know. It follows that the mystic life is reserved to those who can lead it, but unlike all other sciences the only technique connected with it is the technique of love; the apprenticeship is that of love; the science is love; and the end is love's guerdon. All this being so, I am sure that there are more true mystics than we can dream, and yet they are few enough. They will grow from more to more, for love always conquers. But as to when this science of love can appeal to all classes I make no pretense of knowing: it is for those who are able to acquire it; and so are the questions answered.

A Brief Note About Max Heindel

Max Heindel was a Christian occultist, astrologer and mystic, perhaps best known for his book, The Rosicrucian Cosmo-Conception. Through his associations with C. W. Leadbeater, he developed a growing interest in the Theosophical Society, so much so that he would go on to become vice president of the organization's Los Angeles chapter. A few years later, while traveling in Germany, he was initiated as a Rosicrucian by an etheric being identifying itself as an "Elder Brother of the Rosicrucian Order." Heindel returned to America, and a year later, in 1909, he founded the organization known as the Rosicrucian Fellowship. For a decade, until his death in 1919, he wrote and published letters once a month, which were mailed to his students. This is one example of his monthly lessons.

Keynote of the Rosicrucian Teachings

by Max Heindel

The burden of last month's lesson was that it is our duty to pass on the fruits of our study in an endeavor to benefit the world. But mystics usually stand aloof from their fellows and the world looks askance at us and our beliefs. This ought not to be, and analysis will prove that the teachings objected to are relatively unimportant and that the most vital of the teachings will find ready acceptance and prepare the way for further instructions.

The value of any particular teaching depends upon its power to make men better *here* and *now*; to make them kind and considerate at home, conscientious in business, loyal to friends, forgiving to enemies; and any teaching which is easily applied, and will accomplish such results, need no further recommendation.

Where shall we look for such a teaching? We have a monumental cosmogony, describing world periods, revolutions, epochs, and races. Will that study make men more kind? Or, if we can get them to pore over the mystery of numbers and names in the Kabala, will they become more conscientious? Surely not; therefore such knowledge is of minor import. Will it make men moral if we teach them of involution and evolution, or if we describe the cyclic journey of the soul through purgatory and heaven? It will not necessarily, at least till we have convinced them that under the Law of Consequence we are subject to rebirth, and reap as we sow. Even a hint of such a belief, however, would turn most people from us.

But, you will ask, what then is left of our teachings? The greatest teaching of all and the most practical. One that will arouse no antagonism in any devotee of any religion, or even in an agnostic, for it need not be labeled religious. It will produce most beneficent results from the day it is applied, and affect future lives also, regardless of whether the man who practices it ever hears the word Rosicrucian or learns more of our teachings.

If you want to really work in God's vineyard--the world--don't isolate yourself. Abstract study may be good part of the time, but go out in the world; win the confidence of people in church, club, or shop. If you set a good example, they will inquire the secret, and you will be privileged to give them the greatest teaching ever known: *The Secret of Soul Growth*.

You may talk to them something like this:

"Every night when I have gone to bed I review the happenings of the day *in reverse order*. I try to judge myself impartially. I blame where blame is due, repent, and resolve to reform. I praise myself, if praise is merited, and determine to do better the next day.

"I fail often to keep my good resolutions, *but I keep on trying*, and little by little I succeed."

It may be well to explain that by reviewing events in reverse order they are more firmly implanted in the memory, but further elucidation should be avoided until you are certain your friend is seeking a solution to the problem of life.

Preface to the Magical Evocation of Apollonius of Tyana

by Madame Blavatsky

We have already said that in the Astral Light, the images of persons and things are preserved. It is also in this light that can be evoked the forms of those who are no longer in our world, and it is by its means that are effected the mysteries of necromancy which are as real as they are denied.

The Cabalists, who have spoken of the spirit-worlds, have simply related what they have seen in their evocations.

Eliphas Levi Zahed (these Hebrew names translated are Alphonse Louis Constant), who writes this book, has evoked and he has seen.

Let us first tell what the masters have written of their visions or intuitions in what they call the light of glory.

The Magical Evocation of Apollonius of Tyana

by Eliphas Levi

We read in the Hebrew book, the "Revolution of the Souls", that there are souls of three kinds: the daughters of Adam, the daughters of the angels, and the daughters of sin. There are also, according to the same book, three kinds of spirits: captive spirits, wandering spirits, and free spirits. Souls are sent in couples; there are, however, souls of men which are born single and whose mates are held captive by Lilth and Noemah, the queens of Strygis; these are the souls which have to make future expiations for their rashness, in assuming a vow of celibacy. For example, when a man renounces from childhood the love of woman, he makes the spouse who was destined for him the slave of the demons of lust. Souls grow and multiply in heaven as well as bodies upon earth. The immaculate souls are the offspring of the union of the angels.

Nothing can enter into heaven except that which is of heaven. After death, then, the divine spirit which animated the man returns alone to heaven, and leaves upon earth and in the atmosphere two corpses. One terrestrial and elementary; the other aerial and sidereal; the one lifeless already, the other still animated by the universal movement of the soul of the world (Astral Light), but destined to die gradually, absorbed by the astral powers which produced it. The earthly corpse is visible: the other is invisible to the eyes of the terrestrial and living body, and cannot be perceived except by the influences of the astral or trans lucid light, which communicates its impressions to the nervous system, and thus affects the organ of sight, so as to make it see the forms which are preserved and the words which are written in

When a man has lived well, the astral corpse or spirit evaporates like a pure incense, as it mounts towards the higher regions; but if man has lived in crime, his astral body, which holds him prisoner, seeks again the objects of passion and desires to resume its course of life. It torments the dreams of young girls, bathes in the steam of spilt blood, and hovers about the places where the pleasures of its life flitted by; it watches continually over the treasures which it possessed and concealed; it exhausts itself in unhappy efforts to make for itself material organs and live evermore. But the stars attract and absorb it; it feels its intelligence weakening, its memory is gradually lost, all its being dissolves, its old vices appear to it as incarnations, and pursue it under monstrous shapes; they attack and devour. The unhappy wretch thus loses successively all the members which served its sinful appetites; then it dies a second time and forever, because it then loses its personality and its memory. Souls which are destined to live, but which are not yet entirely purified, remain for a longer or shorter time captives in the astral body, where they are refined by the Odic light, which seeks to assimilate them to itself and dissolve. It is to rid themselves of this body that suffering souls sometimes enter the bodies of living persons, and remain there for a while in a state which the Cabalists call embryonic.

These are the aerial phantoms evoked by necromancy. These are the larvae, substances dead or dying, with which one places himself in *rapport;* ordinarily they cannot speak except by the ringing in our ears, produced by the nervous quivering of which I have spoken, and usually reasoning only as they reflect upon our thoughts or dreams.

But to see these strange forms one must put himself in

an exceptional condition, partaking at once of sleep and death; that is to say, one must magnetize himself and reach a kind of lucid and wakeful somnambulism.

Necromancy, then, obtains real results, and the evocations of magic are capable of producing veritable apparitions. We have said that in the great magical agent, which is the astral light, are preserved all the impressions of things, all the images formed, either by their rays or by their reflections; it is in this light that our dreams appear to us, it is this light which intoxicates the insane and sweeps away their enfeebled judgment into the pursuit of the most fantastic phantoms. To see without illusions in this light it is necessary to push aside the reflections by a powerful effort of the will, and draw to oneself only the rays. To dream waking is to see in the astral light; and the orgies of the witches' Sabbath, described by so many sorcerers upon their criminal trials, did not present themselves to them in any other manner. Often the preparations and the substances employed to arrive at this result were horrible, as we have seen in the chapters devoted to the Ritual; but the results were never doubtful. Things of the most abominable, fantastic and impossible description were seen, heard and touched.

In the spring of the year 1854 I went to London to escape from certain family troubles and give myself up, without interruption, to science. I had introductory letters to eminent persons interested in supernatural manifestations. I saw several, and found in them, combined with much politeness, a great deal of indifference or frivolity. Immediately they demanded of me miracles, as they would of a charlatan. I was a little discouraged, for to tell the truth, far from being disposed to initiate others into the mysteries of ceremonial magic, I have always dreaded for myself the illusions and fatigues thereof; besides, these ceremonies demand materials at once expensive and hard to collect together. I, therefore, buried myself in the study of the High Cabala, and thought no more of the English adepts until one day, upon entering my lodging, I found a note with my address. This note contained the half of a card, cut in two, and upon which I recognized at once the character of Solomon's seal, and a very small bit of paper, upon which was written in pencil: "Tomorrow, at three o'clock, before Westminster Abbey, the other half of this card will be presented you". I went to this singular rendezvous. A carriage was standing at the place. I held in my hand, with seeming indifference, my half of the card; a servant approached, and opening the carriage door, made me a sign. In the carriage was a lady in black, whose bonnet was covered with a very thick veil; she beckoned to me to take a seat beside her, at the same time showing me the other half of the card which I had received. The footman closed the door, the carriage rolled away; and the lady having raised her veil I perceived a person whose eyes were sparkling and extremely piercing in expression. "Sir", said she to me, with a very strong English accent, "I know that the law of secrecy is very rigorous among adepts; a friend of Sir Bulwer Lytton, who has seen you, knows that experiments have been requested of you, and that you have refused to satisfy their curiosity. Perhaps you have not the necessary things: I wish to show you a complete magic cabinet; but I demand of you in advance the most inviolable secrecy. If you do not give this promise upon your honor I shall order the coachman to reconduct you to your house". I promised what was required, and I show my fidelity in mentioning neither the name, the quality, nor the residence of this lady, whom I soon recognized as an initiate, not precisely of the first degree, but of a very high one. We had long conversations, in the course of which she constantly insisted upon the necessity of practical experiments to complete initiation. She showed me a collection of magical robes and instruments, even lent me some curious books that I needed; in short, she decided to try at her house the experiment of a complete evocation, for which I prepared myself during twenty-one days, by scrupulously observing the practices indicated in the 24th chapter of the Ritual.

All was ready by the 24th of July; our purpose was to evoke the phantom of the Divine Apollonius and interrogate him as to two secrets, of which one concerned myself and the other interested this lady. She had at first intended to assist at the evocation, with an intimate friend; but at the last moment her courage failed, and, as three persons or one are strictly required for magical rites, I was left alone. The cabinet prepared for the evocation was arranged in the small tower, four concave mirrors were properly disposed, and there was a sort of altar, whose white marble top was surrounded by a chain of magnetized iron. Upon the white marble was chiseled and gilded the sign of the Pentagram; and the same sign was traced in different colors upon a fresh white lambskin, which was spread under the altar. In the center of the marble slab there was a little brazier of copper, containing charcoal of elm and laurel wood; another brazier was placed before me, on a tripod. I was clothed in a white robe, something like those used by our Catholic priests, but longer and more full, and I wore upon my head a crown of verbena leaves interwoven in a golden chain. In one hand I held a naked sword and in another the *Ritual*. I lighted the two fires with the substance requisite and prepared, and I began at first in a low voice; then louder by degrees, the invocations of the *Ritual*. The smoke spread, the flame flickered and made to dance all the objects it lighted, then went out. The smoke rose white and slow from the marble altar. It seemed to me as if I had detected a slight shock of earthquake, my ears rang and my heart beat rapidly. I added some twigs and perfumes to the brazier, and when the flame rose I saw distinctly, before the altar, a human figure, larger than life-size, which decomposed and melted away. I recommenced the evocations, and placed myself in a circle which I had traced in advance of the ceremony between the altar and the tripod; I saw then the disk of the mirror facing me, and behind the altar became illuminated by degrees, and a whitish form there developed itself, enlarging and seeming to approach little by little. I called three times upon Apollonius, at the same time closing my eyes; and, when I re-opened them, a man was before me, completely enveloped in a shroud, which seemed to me rather gray than white; his face was thin, sad and beardless, which did not seem to convey to me the idea, which I had previously formed of Apollonius. I experienced a sensation of extraordinary cold, and when I opened my mouth to question the phantom, it was impossible for me to articulate a sound. I then put my hand upon the sign of the Pentagram, and I directed towards him the point of the sword, commanding him mentally by that sign not to frighten me but to obey. Then the form became confused and suddenly disappeared. I commanded it to re-appear; upon which I felt pass near me, like a breath, and something having touched the hand which touched the sword, I felt my arm instantly stiffened as far as the shoulder. I thought I understood that this sword offended the spirit, and I planted it by the point in the circle near me. The human figure then reappeared, but I felt such a weakness in my limbs, and such a sudden exhaustion seize hold of me, that I took a couple of steps to seat myself. As soon as I was in my chair, I fell into a profound slumber, accompanied by dreams, of which, upon returning to myself, I had only a vague and confused remembrance. For several days my arm was stiff and painful. The apparition had not spoken to me, but it seemed that the questions which I wished to ask it answered themselves in my mind. To that of the lady an interior voice replied in me, "Dead!" (it concerned a man of whom she wished to have some intelligence). As to myself I wished to know if reconciliation and pardon would be possible between two persons, of whom I thought, and the same interior echo answered pitilessly, "Dead!"

I relate these facts exactly as they happened, not forcing them upon the faith of anyone. The effect of this first experiment upon me was something inexplicable. I was no longer the same man.

I twice repeated, in the course of a few days, the same experiment. The result of these two other evocations was to reveal to me two Cabalistic secrets, which might, if they were known by everyone, change in a short time the foundations and laws of the whole of society. I will not explain by what physiological laws I saw and touched; I simply assert that I did see and touch, that I saw clearly and distinctly, without dreaming, and that is enough to prove the efficacy of magic ceremonies.

I will not close this chapter without noticing the curious beliefs of certain Cabalists, who distinguish apparent from real death, and think that they seldom occur simultaneously. According to their story, the greatest part of persons buried are alive, and many others, whom we think living, are in fact dead. Incurable insanity, for existence, would be, according to them, an incomplete but real death, which leaves the earthly body under the exclusive instinctive control of the astral or sidereal body. When the human soul experiences a shock too violent for it to bear, it would separate itself from the body and leave in its place the animal soul, or, in other words, the astral body; which makes of the human wreck something in one sense less living than even an animal. Dead persons of this kind can be easily recognized by the complete extinction of the affectional and moral senses; they are not bad, they are not good; they are dead. These beings, who are the poisonous mushrooms of the human species, absorb as much as they can of the vitality of the living; that is why their approach paralyzes the soul, and sends a chill to the heart. These corpse-like beings prove all that has ever been said of the vampires, those dreadful creatures who rise at night and suck the blood from the healthy bodies of sleeping persons. Are there not some beings in whose presence one feels less intelligent, less good, often even less honest? Does not their approach quench all faith and enthusiasm, and do they not bind you to them by your weaknesses, and enslave you by your evil inclinations, and make you gradually lose all moral sense in a constant torture?

These are the dead whom we take for living persons; these are the vampires whom we mistake for friends!

Postscript to the Magical Evocation of Apollonius of Tyana

by Madame Blavatsky

So little is known in modern times of Ancient Magic, its meaning, history, capabilities, literature, adepts and results, that we cannot allow what precedes to go out, without a few words of explanation. The ceremonies and paraphernalia so minutely described by Levi, are calculated and were intended to deceive the superficial reader. Forced by an irresistible impulse to write what he knew, but fearing to be dangerously explicit, in this instance, as everywhere throughout his works, he magnifies unimportant details and slurs over things of greater moment. True, Oriental Occultists need no preparation, no costumes, apparatus, coronets or warlike weapons; for these appertain to the Jewish Kabala, which bears the same relation to its simple Chaldean prototype as the ceremonious observances of the Roman Church to the simple worship of Christ and his apostles. In the hands of the true adepts of the East, a simple wand of bamboo, with seven joints, supplemented by their ineffable wisdom and indomitable willpower, suffices to evoke spirits and produce the miracles authenticated by the testimony of a cloud of unprejudiced witnesses. At this *séance* of Levi's, upon the reappearance of the phantom, the daring investigator saw and heard things which, in his account of the first trial, are wholly suppressed, and in that of the others merely hinted at. We know this from authorities not to be questioned.

Simon Magus

by Jules Doinel

The Magus of Samaria is the first doctor of the Gnosis. His teaching contains the germ of that grand philosophy which we, towards the end of this nineteenth century, after an eclipse of several hundred years, recognize as the most perfect and luminous expression of the absolute.

I say an eclipse, but in reality the Gnosis has never been without its disciples and its apostles. Both, through persecution and what is even worse, ridicule, have been obliged to protect themselves by maintaining an inviolable silence, wrapped in the obscurity of uncomprehended symbols.

A sovereign interest draws us towards the high priest of Samaria. Not that he has invented the Gnosis, for it was taught under another form in the temples of Egypt, in India and Chaldea, the Gnosis being in fact as old as the Truth, of which it is the mystic garment. But Simon was the first to draw up its dogmas in their esoteric shape, and he is, as his name indicates, the ancestor, the first parent of the Gnosis posterior to Jesus Christ.

He was born at Gitta in Samaria, which, proud of his celebrity, called him the Great Virtue of God. After having lived at Tyre, where he met Helen, his lovely and mysterious companion, he went to Rome and for a time rivaled the renown of the Apostle Peter.

Simon was deeply versed in Oriental and Greek culture. Empedocles and Stesichorus were known to him, and he also was imbued with the ideal philosophy of Plato. A contemporary of Philo the Jew, he had frequented the school of Theosophy at Alexandria. He knew anatomy, having written a celebrated treatise on the circulation of the blood and the physical system of the female body. He was equally well grounded in practical Theurgy. Magus, litterateur, physiologist, mathematician and orator, this great man was cut out for the performance of some special mission.

Already celebrated in the early days of Christianity, Simon devoted to the service of the Gnosis a soul grandly simple and single-minded and of the purest honesty.

Many even of his enemies have been obliged to acknowledge this, and M. Amelineau proves this to be the case in his book on *"Gnosticisme Egyptien"*. Simon, being present at the wonders worked by the deacon Philip, asked to be baptized. Like all Initiates, he only saw in this ceremony a form of initiation. He in no wise pretended to turn from the Gnosis.

In the request he made to Peter to confer upon him the Holy Ghost by the placing of hands, he never recognized a departure from his original principles. Nor did he offer money to buy the Holy Ghost, as the ignorant and the malicious say, but simply the customary and legal price of initiative societies for the possession of the symbolical degree, which he wished to obtain. A European adept would act in a precisely similar manner, if he wished to be admitted to mysteries which were still unknown to him. In the division which subsequently took place between the apostles and the magi, the former were in the wrong, and Simon gives a touching example of his humility and gentleness in the words he addressed to the dark and bigoted Cephas: *"Pray for me, so that nothing of that which you predict for me may happen"*.

Tradition says that Simon of Gitta made the acquaintance of Helen in a brothel; that he reclaimed her and placed her amongst the initiated. But there is a great deal more than this meant by the tradition, for she was to him the symbol and living image of the fall of thought into matter. Nobly as was possible to such a man, did he love this woman, and she requited his love with marvelous intelligence and profound affection for him.

We know nothing as to his death. The fables which are told concerning his end being apocryphal inventions of narrow-minded Christians, based on the theurgical power of levitation often possessed by theosophical adepts.

Simon wrote the "*Anthiretica*" and the Great "*Apophasis*" of which the author of "*Philosophumena*" has preserved some fragments. By the aid of these we may obtain a fairly correct idea of the doctrine of the Samaritan doctor. The Gnosis claims to explain everything. It is active in every department of human thought, being equally concerned with that which belongs to heaven as with that which is of the earth. The Gnosis, as its name shows, is *Knowledge*. God, man, the world, are the trinity of which it is the grand synthesis.

Simon Magus places Fire at the beginning, Fire having been the first cause of the cosmos. God, says the initiate Moses, is a consuming fire. This fire, very different from the earthly fire, which is merely its symbol, has a visible and a hidden existence. Its occult and secret essence hides itself behind its material manifestation or visible appearance; which latter again withdraws itself into its hidden essence. In other words, the invisible is visible to the initiate while the visible is invisible to the profane, which means that the profane are unable to recognize the spirit, disguised under its outward form: the Vedas taught in earlier times this original dogma when they treated of Agni, the supreme fire. This fire of Simon is the same as that of Empedocles; it is that of the fire-worshippers of Iran. It is the burning thicket of Genesis. It represents the Intelligible and the Sensible of the divine Plato, the Power and the Act of the profound Aristotle; and it is also the flaming star of the masonic Lodges.

In the external manifestation of the primordial fire we have all the seeds of matter, while its interior manifestation evolves the world of spirit. So that this fire containing the absolute and the relative, matter and spirit, is at once multiple and one, or God and that which emanates from God. This fire, the eternal cause of all, expands by emanation. It is eternally becoming. But while developing, it itself remains stable and permanent. It is in fact that which is, has been, and shall be, the immovable, the infinite, the substance of all.

But while this immutable it is not inert, the Infinite may act because it is intelligence and reason. From the potential it passes to the active, and thought becomes an expression: the word. Thus Intelligence becomes aware of itself and by so doing acts, evolves, emanates. In formulating its thought, Intelligence unites the moments of this thought and binds its ideas one to another by the tie of reason, and as two comes from one, because one in emanating must become two, fire emanates by couples, of which one is active, the other passive, one male, the other female, one *he* and one *she*. The Gnosis calls this two-fold emanation the Eons. Thus the sphere of the absolute, the superior world, was peopled by six Eons, or six first emanations from God. Simon called them Nous and Ennoia (*spirit and thought*), Phone and Onoma (*the word and the name*), Logismos and Enthumesis (*reasoning and reflection*), and in each of these six emanations is God in a potential state.

"*In each of these roots*", said the Sage, "*the Infinite Power was in its entirety. It had to be formulated by a shape in order that it might appear in all its essence, virtue, grandeur, and effects so that the emanations would become equal to the infinite and eternal Power. If on the other hand it were not to be manifested by a form, the Power could not become active and would be lost for want of being used; just as a man who having an aptitude for grammar and geometry, if it is not used obtains no sort of benefit from it and it becomes lost to him and he is just as if he had never had those powers.*"

By this Simon meant that the Eons in order to be God-like must create. So that just as God passed from the potential to the active state, so the Eons must do likewise. And this is required by the divine law of analogy, and thus the six first emanations became the cause of six new emanations.

The Syzygies, like the six first, continued to emanate male and female, active and passive entities. "It is written", says Simon, "that there are two kinds of Eons having neither beginning nor end and issuing from one common root, the Silence (*the great Sige*) which is the invisible and incomprehensible power", one of these seems superior to the other; it is the great Power characterized as the Intelligence of all things; it orders everything and is male and positive, the other is inferior and is called the great Thought or female Eon. These two Eons are complementary and manifest between them the middle region, the incomprehensible air, which has had neither beginning nor end.

See what a wonderful picture is presented to us in the divine ladder, which Jacob saw in a dream as he slept with his head pillowed on the sacred stone of Bethel beneath the starry firmament, which spanned the Desert. The Eons mount and descend this most mysterious ladder in pairs and constitute the links in the chain, which stretches from God to Earth and back again to God, arid each two are male and female, associated forms or united thoughts. They weave the woof of spirit and of matter, realizing God in things and carrying these back again into God, and the law, которая knits and directs them elevates and abases them and works as the sacred and primordial fire which, as God, is infinite and absolute and as expressing, which in its highest expression may be called Love.

Next Simon opens to us the second world. It is peopled by six Eons, the reflection of the first six and bearing the same names.

The incomprehensible air or second world is inhabited by the Father, he who is, was and shall be, without beginning or end, male and female living in one unity. He develops in the same way as the fire of the first world, for he manifests by the power of thought. The Father, which is the Power, and the *thought* which it produces, are complementary, being in reality one, as represented in the male which envelopes the female, the Spirit in the idea, or Nous in the Epinoia. In other words, the Spirit has a thought, which it proclaims by the word or the name Father. This Father is also silence.

Epinoia, the female Eon, enticed by love, leaves the Father and emanates angels and powers from which proceed the world which we live in. These angels, forgetting the existence of the Father, have wished to keep amongst themselves Epinoia, and from this cause we have their fall and the necessity for a redemption.

Man is the product of one of these angels, the Demiurgus, which the Bible calls God. By him man is made double, after his own image and appearance. The image is the spirit, which circles the waters of the abyss of which Genesis speaks. *Spiritus Dei ferebatur super aquas.* Man is an Eon, because in him there is the likeness of the Father, and like the Father, he will produce other beings. He will in fact reproduce himself.

This brings us to the anthropological doctrine of the Samaritan Magus. Fire is the principle of the act of generation, for to desire to be united to a woman is called "to be on fire". This fire is one in itself but double in its effects. Man transmits in the seed the hot red blood, while the woman becomes the laboratory where the blood is turned into milk. It was thus that the sword of Fire, which flashed before the gates of Eden in the hands of the Archangel typified by the quivering of its living flame the transformation of blood into seed and milk. Without this circulation of blood the tree of Life would die and the icy hand of death would congeal the World.

Continuing his subtle and profound analysis, Simon explained the development of the fetus after its conception.

Interpreting the words addressed to Jeremiah, "I have formed thee in the bosom of thy mother", he explained that man in Eden meant the fetus in the matrix, and he saw in the four rivers, which fertilized the terrestrial paradise the ducts, which adhere to the child and bring him nourishment.

How strange and original a conception of a great mind is this inspiration of genius drawn from the physiological meditations of a superior man in a primitive age. Let us now return to Epinoia, which the Angels, the ancestors of man, have retained captive. The Power of Thought drawn backwards by its celestial instincts is ever sighing after Sige and striving to return to the Father. The Angels hold it fast, however, and make it suffer that they may keep it amongst them, and finally they succeed in imprisoning it in a human body. This is the commencement of that long pilgrimage which the divine exile makes through a series of transmigrations and long ages of suffering. This fall of Intellect into matter is the origin of evil. It is forfeiture and to such there must be redemption; Epinoia transmigrates from woman to woman through the ages like a scent, which passes from vase to vase. The day on which Simon penetrated into the Syrien den he met the migratory "thought" in the form of this Helen, of this prostitute whom he loved and whom he transfigured by his love. Loving her he applied with practical exactness the parable of the lamb, who was lost and found. Thus runs the allegory. Just as Simon saved Helen from final degradation in taking her from the slough into which she had fallen, the Savior sent by the Father descended to the world and delivered Thought from the tyranny of the lower Angels. In order to accomplish this act of infinite love Soter, the Savior, the Son left the One, the Silence, the Fire, and passed through the first world down to the second where he incarnated in the world of Bodies, burying himself in the Astral Form or Perispirit. In Judea he was called the Son. In Samaria the Samaritans called him the Father. With the Gentiles he was the Holy Ghost. He was in fact the Great Virtue of God and Simon Magus knew himself in Him.

Just as Simon set himself to seek Helen, so the Savior seeks the human Soul. He found her in a house of ill-fame, that is to say in Evil, and as Simon married Helen so the Savior married the Soul. "In truth", says the wise Amelineau, "*this myth of Epinoia is very beautiful. The divine Thought held in bondage by inferior beings who owe it their very life and who wish to become its equal; degraded by these Angels and debased to the lowest degree, it forms a sublime allegory of the futile efforts of the human soul struggling towards God, of which it is the image, and falling from one abyss to another, from crime to crime, held in control by jealous spirits who, full of envy, endeavor to impede its upward progress towards him whom it resembles?"*.

Each one of us, for we are Eons, may become the Simon to a Helen or, reversing the parts, a Helen to a Simon. In order to fulfill our mission of Savior, we, the initiates of the Gnosis, must appear to the profane as similar in form to them but their superior in spirit. Simon and Helen have taught us, and we in our turn must teach, the liberating power of the Gnosis, the illuminating science, the law or the lost Word of the Rosicrucians. We will deliver our brothers and our sisters from the yoke of ignorance and superstition, of gross materialism and haughty skepticism. We will dress them in the white robes of Initiation. No matter where the seed is sown, so long as it is sown; saved by the Gnosis we become saviors, happy if we possess, perhaps not the genius of Simon Magus, but his great heart and wide charity.

Introduction to the Emerald Tablet

Perhaps most known for the philosophical axiom "as above, so below," the Emerald Tablet of Hermes, more traditionally known as the Smaragdine Table, was revered for purporting to contain the secret of the philosopher's stone.

While traditionally attributed to the Hellenistic and syncretic combination of the Greek god Hermes and the Egyptian god Thoth, known as Hermes Trismegistus, the earliest surviving text is in Arabic and dates between the sixth and eighth century. The first Latin translation didn't arrive until the twelfth century, and over the years, many notable occultists and hermeticists have translated this short but influential text into English.

Although it is a work of few words and only 14 sentences in length, the Emerald Tablet is considered a corner-stone of Hermetic thought, even inspiring the popular-culture movement based on the 2006 best-selling book, *The Secret*. The translation of the Emerald Tablet presented here is from the pen of Isaac Newton.

The Emerald Tablet

Translated by Isaac Newton

1. Tis true without error, certain & most true.
2. That which is below is like that which is above & that which is above is like that which is below to do the miracles of one only thing
3. And as all things have been & arose from one by the mediation of one: so all things have their birth from this one thing by adaptation.
4. The Sun is its father, the moon its mother, the wind hath carried it in its belly, the earth is its nurse.
5. The father of all perfection in the whole world is here.
6. Its force or power is entire if it be converted into earth.
7. Separate thou the earth from the fire, the subtle from the gross sweetly with great industry.
8. It ascends from the earth to the heaven & again it descends to the earth & receives the force of things superior & inferior.
9. By this means you shall have the glory of the whole world
10. & thereby all obscurity shall fly from you.
11. Its force is above all force. For it vanquishes every subtle thing & penetrates every solid thing.
12. So was the world created.
13. From this are & do come admirable adaptations whereof the means (or process) is here in this. Hence I am called Hermes Trismegistus, having the three parts of the philosophy of the whole world
14. That which I have said of the operation of the Sun is accomplished & ended.

The Reality of the Astral Plane

Part I

by C. W. Leadbeater

To speak about the astral plane in India is a somewhat different thing from speaking about it in other lands. In England or in America the great difficulty which the ordinary auditor finds with regard to the matter is to believe that there is any condition beyond the physical. Although the religion of those countries teaches quite as decidedly (although *not as accurately*) as yours that there is another state of existence, a state after death, yet unfortunately the statements made about it by their churches and in their sacred books are put in such an unscientific manner that the trend of modern thought (which *is, as you know, along more or less precise and scientific lines*) leads people practically to reject all that is said about the unseen world. Again and again I have lectured on such subjects in many places; again and again newspaper editors, in commenting upon what I have said, have remarked that it was most reasonable, that in every way it seemed exactly what it ought to be - and yet they invariably concluded by saying, "But of course it is absolutely impossible that anybody really can know anything about these matters." In fact, they seem to think that although Theosophical teaching may be what they call in Italy, well invented, it cannot really mean anything or be anything more than a brilliant hypothesis.

Now I take it that that is not in the least the difficulty which will beset an Indian audience with regard to this matter. You all know from ancient teaching that there is an unseen world - that there is very much existing about us and acting about us all the time, of which our physical senses bring us no report whatever. You are all aware of that, and you do not need any further proof of it; or if there should be any of you who do, they must be the products of half- assimilated western education. There are, however, some difficulties in the minds of many Hindus with regard to the astral plane and the Theosophical teaching concerning it. I have met at different times with two classes of objections in this country, and I should like to say a word about them.

The Reality of the Astral Plane

Part II:

Should the Astral Plane be Studied?

First, it is considered by some Indians that although the astral plane exists, it is yet a thing about which we should think as little as possible. There is such a place, of course, and we must pass through its conditions, but our duty is to fix our thoughts upon the very highest ideal that we can reach, to strain upwards towards that, and not to contemplate any of these lower and intermediate conditions. With part of that I perfectly agree. It is true that every man should set before himself constantly the highest ideal which he is capable of forming. It is unquestionably well that his thoughts should be aimed at that ideal, and that it should influence him in all his actions and through the whole course of his life. But we have this to remember. We are here in the physical world and our duty at the present moment is largely connected with that world. We are in this physical body precisely in order that we may learn lessons through it. If we had no lessons to learn on this material level, we should already have transcended it and we should not need any further incarnation here. So it cannot be argued that in keeping before ourselves the highest ideal we ought to ignore life on the physical plane.

You may say that to some extent the hermit does ignore this lower world, but that is not the usual course. If a man's karma be such that he can legitimately tear himself away from everything physical and go away and live in a cave or in a jungle and devote himself utterly to the contemplation of the highest, that man is already in the fortunate position of being able largely to leave the physical plane out of his calculations. But you all know well that for the enormous majority of you such a way as that is not possible. You may be just as highly developed or as good as the hermit, but you have plain and obvious duties which nothing would justify your discarding. That being so, it is clear that some knowledge of the physical world is of value to you. A teacher who told you to keep your mind fixed only on Nirvanic conditions and to learn nothing about the surroundings of daily life and the temptations which you may meet, would manifestly not be a practical guide.

I should submit, in answer to the objection which I mentioned to you at the beginning, that for the great majority of us a certain amount of life upon the astral plane is a necessity for our evolution. If we have not yet transcended the physical, still less have we transcended this higher realm of Nature, and it is inevitable that many of us should have considerable experiences in connection with the astral plane. Remember that we pass at least one-fourth of our lives, and in many cases one-third, in the sleep of the physical body, and that during that time the consciousness of the man is not asleep, but is active in another vehicle and on another plane of matter. A condition in which we spend at least one quarter of our life is hardly one that is well for us entirely to ignore; and we must also remember that after casting aside our physical bodies we shall most of us pass some considerable time in this astral world, so that it cannot be entirely unimportant to know what we may with regard to it.

There is yet another consideration. Many of us are trying to utilize some powers a little higher than the physical, such as the power of thought, and the power of strong, loving, helpful emotion. If these are to be used efficiently, some knowledge of the material through which they work is required - some knowledge of the conditions under which they are to be employed. I do not say that without such knowledge it would be impossible to produce any result, but I do say that it would be achieved somewhat blindly and that much of the effort would be wasted; whereas with some comprehension of the laws of this higher side of our world it is less likely that strength will be squandered uselessly and valuable time lost. In order that we may help forward the evolution of the world while our physical bodies are in a state of rest, or after they have been cast aside, we must have some knowledge of the subject. It is true that there are certain fascinations connected with the astral world - possibilities of selfishness and sensuality of various kinds; and those who enter upon astral life may quite conceivably be entangled in such snares, and thus delayed in their progress. But each many will necessarily have some contact with astral life whether he knows anything about it or not; and the more he knows about it, the better he understands it, the more likely will he be to avoid mistakes.

Never for one moment have any of our writers suggested to any person that he should set before him astral life as a goal at which to aim. We have consistently said, "Always set the very highest before you as the goal; but since you have to live on the physical plane, recognize the fact and try to understand that, after all, the physical world also is a manifestation of the Supreme, that the astral world is simply nothing but the continuation of the physical world in finer matter, and that you may study the astral conditions of matter precisely as you study etheric conditions of matter, by applying to them scientific methods of research." That is the way in which we have been approaching this matter, both in writing and in lecturing; and I do not think that any Indian who really understands our attitude will take exception to it.

The Reality of the Astral Plane

Part III:

Is Our Description Accurate?

Another objection which I have heard in India is of a different character. There are many Indian teachers who know of the existence of the astral plane, but they say that the accounts of it which they find in Theosophical books do not agree with their own experiences of it. That is a legitimate objection, and it is quite easy for us from our standpoint to understand the position of the man who makes it; but I think that from his standpoint he cannot find it easy to understand our position unless he supposes us the victims of some kind of gigantic hallucination. Now undoubtedly a man may become a victim of illusion, and he may carry on for a long time the same line of illusions, and may live among the thought-forms thus created; and a scheme resting upon the vision of a single person might quite conceivably be accounted for in this way. But while I at least have never asked any human being to believe anything because I have seen it or because I know it, I do think that what has been written in Theosophical literature with regard to the astral plane and to the life and work upon that plane is very fairly well established, by reason of the fact that that is the nearest plane in consciousness to the physical, and that, therefore, we have a considerable number of persons who have had at least occasional experiences in connection with it, and a smaller number for whom it is a prominent part of regular daily life, to whom it is just as familiar as are the streets of your city to you.

If you speak of statements concerning some very high

plane which only a few have as yet been able to touch in consciousness, then naturally you have for them so much the less of testimony, for that plane is necessarily much further removed from the physical, and therefore fewer experiments have been made in connection with it. In that case an objector would have more justification in holding that perhaps there might be errors in matters so far beyond ordinary consciousness. But when we are dealing with a band of investigators, people of different races, of varying temperaments and types, and when, in spite of all these differences, they broadly agree as to what they see and how they see it, when they constantly meet in that condition of consciousness, the memory of which is often transferred to the physical plane on opposite sides of the world, it will be readily understood that for those people themselves there grows to be a strong conviction that they are not hallucinated when they believe themselves to be using a consciousness somewhat more extended than that of the average man, and they are consequently quite undisturbed by the criticism of men who have not studied the subject. Those of us who have enquired into the matter have a huge mass of evidence that the astral plane is a reality and that clairvoyance is a fact, and that by means of this faculty we have gained much information which we have put before our brothers in order that they may also have the benefit which such knowledge has brought to us.

I have heard it said here in India that no one ought to give a lecture or write a book on these subjects until he has attained Adeptship, because short of that there must be imperfection. That is quite true; but I would suggest that if our revered founder, Madame Blavatsky, had followed that advice and had waited for the attainment of perfect Adeptship before writing anything, we should not have had "The Secret Doctrine". If Mrs Besant, Mr Sinnett and others had adopted that plan we should have had no Theosophical books for perhaps six or seven thousand years yet, and while the books would undoubtedly have been far more valuable when they came, still the present generation would not have gained the advantage of Theosophical teaching.

We have chosen deliberately to put the imperfect knowledge before our brothers, because we have always felt that such powers come to us not for ourselves only but for them - that we are, so to speak, eyes for our fellows, and we have tried to be faithful eyes. We have tried to report exactly what we have seen, even though we know far better than others what are the difficulties that lie in the way of an accurate report. We know well that you will have very much more to learn as the years roll on, but what we have tried to do, though we may not have wholly succeeded, is to put these things before you in such a manner that as your perceptions widen you will have nothing to unlearn - you will have only to add to your stock of knowledge, and not to alter it. What I think we may hope is that we leave no fundamental principles wrongly stated.

If we consider carefully the astral experiences of many of our Indian friends, and also of some Christian mystics, we shall see that they may readily be harmonized with our own, even though at first sight they seem to differ. It should be remembered that the astral world is as extensive and as varied as the physical world. If visitors from some other planet were to come to this earth and carry back to their own their reports of what they had seen here, it is obvious that twenty of them, or indeed fifty or a hundred of them, might visit different parts of this world, and carry back with them widely differing stories, even though all of them reported accurately the experiences through which they had passed. Exactly in the same way the person who visits the astral plane comes into contact only with a very small part of it, and unless he constantly repeats his visits, and makes systematic efforts to investigate all its varied possibilities, he will naturally return with an exceedingly partial report.

It often happens that by intensity of devotion a man is able to raise his consciousness to the astral level. He forms a strong mental image of the object of his devotional feeling and surrounds himself by a shell that keeps away all other thoughts or vibrations. Thus, even when his consciousness acts through his astral vehicle, it still acts within that shell, and so he sees nothing but the object of his devotion, and is as entirely unaware of the varied life and activity which surrounds him as the ascetic who sits in rapt meditation is unmindful of movements taking place in the physical world around him. We who work on the astral plane constantly see men thus in ecstasy within their own private holy places, created by the intensity of their devotion; and undoubtedly they derive the greatest benefit from such experiences. But they err when they assume that the whole astral world is included in their shell, and that there is nothing to be found there but that which they have seen. This it will be obvious that while their theory of this world of subtle matter leaves them no alternative but to suppose us hallucinated, our theory has the advantage of fully including and explaining their experiences without suggesting any such unpleasant insinuation.

The Reality of the Astral Plane

Part IV:

Its Agreement with the Scriptures

You will observe that in speaking of this subtler world I am using the term "astral plane", and not "Kamaloka", which is often employed as a Sanskrit equivalent. I avoid that because I am not sure that it is an equivalent, for I think that when you define it as the place of desire you mean almost exclusively lower desire, and that would make it much more limited than is the astral plane. I believe that your term "bhuvarloka" is much nearer to a correspondence, but without an exhaustive study of references I dare not pledge myself even to that. The way in which the Indians approach the subject, and the way in which their books are written, are somewhat the reverse of ours. They always descend upon it from above, as it were, and their great Rishis, scheming out the whole plan of the universe, say with the calm certainty of knowledge "Thus it must be".

We, on the other hand, approach the subject from below, and patiently catalogue fact after fact over and over again, venturing to draw our deductions only after comparing the results of varied and oft-repeated experiments and observations. But the point which I think should be of interest to you in India is that although these investigations are made from so different a direction, the results agree precisely with the statements of your ancient books, thus offering a corroboration of the religious teaching which ought specially to appeal to the younger generation because it comes along the very line in which their thought has been trained - the line of scientific enquiry. Another point of interest about the observations of the Theosophical students is that they give, I think, somewhat greater detail than the scriptures, and they arrange their facts in tabular form so that the relation between them can be clearly seen.

If I were asked to teach any one what I know about the astral plane, I think the first thing that I should tell him is that he should get into his mind the utter reality of it. That should be less difficult for an Indian than for a Western audience. Try to realize that this other condition of existence is just as real (or *just as unreal*) as this. There are philosophers who would say that all existence is illusion - that we ourselves are unreal - that I am deluded when I think I am speaking, and that you are hallucinated when you think you are listening; but however that may be, while we live on this physical plane we have to act as though we were real, and the same thing exactly applies to the astral plane. If this physical world be nothing but an utter delusion, then the same may be true of the astral; but if there be any measure of reality connected with this world in which we are now living, just the same measure of reality belongs to the astral plane also. Remember, I do not mean that either of them is permanent. If you ask whether the physical plane is permanent, I should say "No; the matter of which it is composed is permanent, but not necessarily in this form." All physical matter may become astral matter, all astral matter may become mental matter, and perhaps that is the way in which the Supreme withdraws into Himself. When the scientist is able to examine the atom of the physical plane as it has been examined clairvoyantly, he will find that it is nothing but a vortex center, held in its spiral shape simply by the force flowing through it, just as you may see at the street corner a little whirling column of dust and leaves held in position by the wind circulating through it. The very atom which is at the back of all physical matter is nothing but an ordered aggregation of astral atoms; and if it should please the Logos of our system to withdraw His power, the whole physical world would fall at once into what would be, for us, non-manifestation. That shows you the relation of the astral plane to the physical; it is just as much a material plane - simply another condition of the same matter.

Furthermore, I have constantly to explain in Europe and America that this astral plane is not a place; it is not a heaven far away among the stars, but a condition of matter existing here and now, though unperceived. Astral matter surrounds us at the moment, just as physical matter surrounds us. You are all acquainted with the scientific theory that ether interpenetrates every substance, even the hardest diamond. Just in the same way as ether interpenetrates ordinary physical matter, so does astral matter in its turn interpenetrate ether. Scientists used to think of the ether as a homogeneous substance; now they appear to admit that it is not so, since they say that everything is constructed of electrons. The truth is that ether is itself atomic, and its atoms do not touch one another, but are floating in a sea of still finer matter, which we call astral. But astral matter in its turn may be reduced until we come to the astral atom; that in its turn is found to be floating in a sea of finer matter still. Now these are not different kinds of matter, but different conditions of the same matter. Some of your magicians have been able to make a physical object disappear from its place and re-appear somewhere else. That is in reality a very simple feat of dematerialization. We may make a block of ice invisible by melting it and then boiling the resulting water; in the form of steam it may be forced through a grating or any porous substance, and, on the other side, if subjected to a sufficiently low temperature, it may again be condensed into an exactly similar block of ice. If this could be done rapidly enough the transfer of the block of ice from one chamber to another would seem miraculous; and this is a precise analogy to what takes place in the case of dematerialization. The magician by an effort of his trained will simply reduces the object to a state of matter in which it is invisible to our senses, but it is none the less material for that - just as the steam is matter as surely as the ice. If it is to be called real in one condition it must be called real in the other; if it is to be called unreal in one of these conditions it must also be called unreal in the other.

The Reality of the Astral Plane

Part V:

What is Reality?

Some of you may find it helpful if you recollect that things are real or unreal to us according to the place in which our consciousness is focused. While our consciousness is focused in the physical brain, physical matter alone is perceptible to us, and so it alone seems real, and although we are living in the midst of the astral world at this moment, to most of us it is unreal because it is imperceptible. A few hours later we shall fall asleep, and our consciousness will change its focus from the physical body to the astral body. Then it will be from astral objects alone that we shall be able to receive vibrations, and so those will seem perceptible and real, and the physical objects, though of course they still surround us as before, will be invisible and will therefore seem unreal. But it is not the condition of things which has changed, it is simply the focus of our consciousness. These physical objects are after all manifestations of the Logos on this plane, and they remain manifestations even when we no longer see them. We are not justified, therefore, in saying that all these things are unreal because it is possible for us to raise our consciousness to a higher level. In that case it is our consciousness that has been modified, not His manifestation.

The Reality of the Astral Plane

Part VI:

The Results of Vibration

If we take up a modern book on physics, we shall find that it usually gives us a table of octaves of vibration, and we cannot but be struck by the fact that only a very small proportion of them appeal to our senses at all. Since all the information that we possess with regard to the outer world has reached us by means of the very few vibrations to which we are normally able to respond, it is abundantly obvious that the clairvoyant who learns to be sensitive to the whole of this part of the gamut will gain a vast amount of additional knowledge about the world in which he lives.

We shall notice that the slower rates of vibration (such *as sound-waves*) affect the comparatively coarse conditions of matter, and set the air in motion; while the more rapid rates (such *as light*) do not affect the air at all, but act upon finer conditions, such as ether. So that when we have realized the existence of astral matter, which is still subtler than the ether, we shall be prepared to find that the forces playing through it are still higher rates of vibration which do not normally affect any physical matter. Investigation shows us that among these higher vibrations are those caused by the desires and emotions of man, and such of his thoughts as are mingled with personal craving or feeling. It is found that such thoughts or emotions are outpourings of energy just as definite as electricity or steam; but this energy acts at its own level and in its own finer type of matter. That is not a mere supposition, but a definite fact observed over and over again by clairvoyant investigators. All the pictures that are drawn for you in our books, illustrating the effects of affection, of devotion or of avarice, are simply the tabulations of observations made upon astral matter - observations which have been repeated many times with substantially the same results. A whole new world is thus opened before us - a world of finer matter pressing upon us on every side; and to this finer type of matter the name "astral" was given by the mediaeval alchemists.

Since this matter surrounds us all the time, in what way is it acting upon us and in what way are we acting upon it? Once more investigate, and you will find that it is constantly reacting upon us, and that we can no more ignore our astral than our physical surroundings. As the world is at present constituted, physical surroundings are by no means unimportant, and we must learn something of the physical world and its forces if we wish to be able to utilize them to help others, or to resist their undue influence upon ourselves. In exactly the same way, if we wish to be able to protect ourselves from undesirable influences from the astral world, and to have its forces at our command for altruistic work, we must study its conditions and its possibilities; for in this case as in every other, knowledge is power.

The Reality of the Astral Plane

Part VII:

The Extension of Knowledge

We find that the laws which govern it are the same with which we are familiar in connection with physical matter - the laws of cause and effect, of action and reaction, and of the conservation of energy; and this fact brings the planes into relation, and shows us that we have to deal not with some strange new world but with another and subtler portion of the old one. The truth is that in studying the astral plane we are simply extending our knowledge of nature a little further in a direction in which it has already been extended more than once. Primitive man, knowing nothing but what was obvious to his senses, can have been aware only of the solid and liquid forms of matter; to him the tempest must have been an inexplicable manifestation of an awful invisible force, and the death which followed the inhalation of noxious fumes must have seemed the mysterious visitation of the deity. Think how great must have been the extension of knowledge and comprehension of nature when from careful observations a theory of gases was deduced, and gradually won its way into universal acceptance! An entirely new realm had opened before those primitive physicists when they thus learnt to study and experiment with this finer condition of matter. A long step further in the same direction was taken when the existence of ether was realized, for by that knowledge many phenomena became explicable which before were deemed miraculous. In earlier days natural laws were but little understood and the world was supposed to be governed by divine caprice; but with each advance of science the domain of law and order was extended, and the unknown outer void in which miracles might happen was decreased. When we suggest the study of the astral plane we are simply recommending another step, but always along the same line of experimenting with ever subtler forms of matter and when this step is taken it will be found that the action of man's thoughts and emotions has been brought within range of law.

The Reality of the Astral Plane

Part VIII:

Theosophy is Advanced Science

In this sense it may accurately be said that the students of Theosophy are the advanced scientists of the day, for they are engaged in examining a field just a little ahead of that which has approved itself to the majority of physicists. Do not forget that our great founder, Madame Blavatsky, displayed a very remarkable knowledge of science, though she does not seem to have learnt it along ordinary lines. She made certain statements in connection with it which were ridiculed at the time, yet the facts which she announced have since been accepted and approved by the most competent authorities. An account of these has been given by Mrs. Besant in "Theosophy and Science", the fourth lecture in "Theosophy applied to Human Life", and Theosophists should familiarize themselves with it. Obviously if one who had not taken up the study of ordinary physical science is yet found to know more of it than its foremost professors knew at the time when she wrote it, it is well worth while to examine what she has said with regard to fields as yet untouched by them.

Science has attained its marvelous results by means of highly perfected instruments; such results as have been attained by the pupils of Madame Blavatsky have been gained in an entirely different way - the way recommended by your teachers of old – the development not of the instrument but of the observer. It is by the employment of that method that Theosophical writers have been able to give you some details of the arrangement of the higher planes and the conditions of life upon them.

I have intentionally avoided the repetition in this lecture of the information as to these conditions which any one who wishes may find in the manual called "The Astral Plane"; instead I have tried to take up the subject with you in its more general aspect in relation to this lower plane, so that you may appreciate the astral as just as much a part of the great world in which we live as is the physical, and may realize that if we want to live wisely and to the best advantage we must endeavor to understand the whole of our world, and not only the lowest part of it.

The Reality of the Astral Plane

Part IX:

How it affects us

This astral world affects us because its vibrations have the same qualities as all other kinds of vibrations - they radiate in all directions, and they tend to reproduce themselves. If two stringed instruments are tuned accurately together, and placed near to one another, it is found that when a note is struck upon one of them, the other vibrates in unison. The vibration of the note radiates in all directions, but when it falls upon something capable of exact response it at once reproduces itself.

If by emotion or passion you set up a vibration in astral matter, it acts in precisely the same way; and necessarily in its radiation it impinges upon the astral bodies of all those about you. If there be among them one which is in tune with that vibration, it will at once be excited to respond to it; that is to say, your emotion will be reproduced in that other man. If, however, that astral body is already pulsating strongly at some different rate, your vibration will not find it in tune, and so cannot affect it. Suppose a man is under the influence of anger, and you are full of gentleness and affection. His astral body is vibrating vigorously at a certain rate; he is in such a condition of palpitation that he does not even feel your gentle radiations; he goes on along his own line, quite uninfluenced by it, just as the man under the sway of wild passion on the physical plane is blind to all suggestions of reason.

The Reality of the Astral Plane

Part X:

The appearance of the Astral Body

People often ask as to the appearance of these astral bodies, and those who have seen one occasionally are sometimes surprised to find that it does not resemble the pictures given in some of our books, such as "Man, Visible and Invisible." They forget that that book was written specially to draw attention to the colors in the luminous ovoid of astral matter, and the effect upon those colors of different emotions and passions, so that a vivid illustration might be given of the way in which man's evolution is affected by the thoughts and feelings of every-day life. Therefore those bodies were drawn, as it were, out of proportion, one part of them being specially emphasized, and another part studiously kept in the background. You may remember that the physical form is outlined in pencil only, in order to show the relative size of the ovoid. In reality that counterpart of the physical body is far more prominent than it is shown in those drawings. It is an exact duplicate of the physical form, perfectly distinct from the surrounding luminous matter, and therefore perfectly recognizable. Every type of physical matter has its corresponding type in astral matter, and the latter is very strongly attracted by the former. There is a counterpart in astral matter for every physical object, and that counterpart is always of suitable type. So that wherever there is solid physical matter it is interpenetrated by astral matter of the lowest sub- plane; where there is physical liquid matter it is interpenetrated by astral matter of the second sub- plane from the bottom; and whether there is physical gas it is interpenetrated by astral matter of the third sub-plane from the bottom, and so on. Just as there is no difficulty in distinguishing a solid object from the air surrounding it on the physical plane, so is there no difficulty in distinguishing its astral counterpart from what we may call the astral air, which surrounds it.

While it is true that a man's astral body takes that ovoid shape which is the visible manifestation, on these lower planes, of the shape of the causal body, it is also true that of the mass of matter contained within that ovoid perhaps ninety-nine per cent is contained within the periphery of the physical form. The reason of this is the very strong attraction exercised by that physical form over the astral matter, and the further fact that when a kind of habit of remaining in a particular form - a sort of momentum of circulation of the astral currents - has been set up, that habit or that momentum will persist for a long time after the cause of it has been withdrawn. Thus although during sleep one leaves his physical body on the bed and moves about in his astral vehicle, the latter continues to retain the exact appearance of the former; and even when the physical body is finally laid aside at death the habit still persists, and the form is still retained through any ordinary length of astral life.

With regard to this matter of appearance there is another point to be borne in mind, and that is that astral matter is far more plastic than physical, and is readily molded by the action of thought. If a man thinks of himself as having a particular form the matter of his astral body will for the moment be molded into that form, and will retain it as long as his thought is firmly fixed upon it; but the moment that he forgets, or his attention is distracted, the astral matter will come under the sway of its habit, and will at once flow back into its natural shape. So that a man can take on any appearance that he pleases, but cannot retain it permanently without devoting the whole of his time to that one thought. Nevertheless a thought, which is almost constantly present in his mind does slowly effect a permanent change. That is true to some extent upon the physical plane; the man who for years leads a debased life presently begins to show signs of it in face and form, while the man who has turned from an evil life to one of purity and holiness presently shows a very decided improvement in physical appearance. Although such a change usually takes places gradually, instances are not wanting in which it has been startlingly rapid. Some cases of what is called "Mind-cure" illustrate this, as does also the appearance of the stigmata upon the bodies of various ecstatics. Madame Blavatsky gives some very remarkable cases of this in "Isis Unveiled". Since astral matter is so much more readily affected than physical, it is comprehensible that a similar change should occur more rapidly in the case of this astral vehicle.

The Reality of the Astral Plane

Part XI:

Suffering After Death

All religions tell us that the conditions of existence after death depend very largely upon the kind of life which the man has led upon the physical plane; that if his life has been good and pure he will find himself happy, but if his earthly course has been gross and evil, trouble and suffering may ensue from it. Unfortunately in some forms of Christian teaching these joys have been regarded as reward and this suffering as punishment; and much grievous misunderstanding has resulted from this clumsy mistake. If in physical life a man seizes hold of a red-hot iron bar his hand will be burnt; but it will hardly occur to him to say that God has punished him for taking hold of that bar. He will say rather that what has happened is the natural result of his own action, and anybody who understands anything of science can explain to him exactly the mechanism of the occurrence, and show him how the intensely rapid vibrations of the hot iron bar have torn apart the tissues of his hand, and so produced what we call a burn. We shall never understand the conditions of life after death until we realize that happiness follows upon good thought or action and suffering upon evil thought or action, in exactly the same way as the burn follows the contact with the hot iron. The cause and its effect are related as the two sides of a coin are related; and just as we cannot draw towards us the obverse side of the coin without also drawing towards us its reverse, so we cannot commit any action or give birth to any thought without at the same time bringing ourselves its result as a definite part of the original action.

The more ignorant among the Christians often speak of the providence of God, and in using that term they mean to imply that the Supreme Being is constantly personally interfering with the working of His own laws, and they usually also imply that He can be induced at their request to exercise such power of interference. This theory also involves the idea that He has originally planned His universe so badly that the machinery needs this constant tinkering in order to make it work satisfactorily - surely not an exalted conception of the Deity. Nothing could be further from the glorious truth, for one of the most striking characteristics of even that small part of the Divine world which we are able to see is its marvelous adaptability and the wonderful elasticity of its action. Men often find it difficult to recognize the accurate working of the law of justice in their own case, even though they cannot but admit that in all the realms of nature there can never be an effect without its appropriate cause.

Common though this position is, we may see its absurdity by taking a very simple analogy. The man who is using an engine expects to get out of it an amount of work proportionate to the amount of energy put into it, say in the form of fuel. He allows for a certain waste from friction, and for a certain amount given off in the form of heat, but still there is a definite proportion of work which he expects to get out of his engine, because he knows that there is a natural law of the conservation of energy. Suppose he should find that he is not getting a proper proportion of work from that engine, we should esteem him a very foolish man if he therefore declared that the law of the conservation of energy was all a delusion and a mistake. If we could suppose him to be so ignorant as to say that his experiment with his machine tended to show that there was no such thing, we should reply that there had been other experiments besides his, and that the law was already established as a definite certainty. It would never occur to the intelligent engineer to doubt for a moment the universal application of that law; he would at once turn to his machine and examine that in order to find the defect which caused the loss of energy. Yet the very same man who is so certain of the inviolability of Nature's law in one direction will begin to grumble about injustice if any suffering or sorrow comes to him; whereas the analogy of his own line of thought with regard to the machine would show that the only sensible conclusion would be that since the law of justice is perfect in its working there must undoubtedly have been something wrong in his own action in the past to account for this sorrow which has fallen upon him.

The Reality of the Astral Plane

Part XII:

The Advantage of the Study

Unquestionably the study of astral and mental forces and of the astral and mental worlds generally helps us to understand how this mighty law of justice produces its results. That is one reason why I think the study of these higher portions of nature so useful to us. It supplements our knowledge of the physical world, and enables us to form a far more complete conception of the whole great scheme, and it is obvious that this wider knowledge must make us of greater use. We see constantly in every-day life that good intentions without knowledge are not sufficient to produce a satisfactory result, for we frequently find that the well-meaning man blunders terribly, and often does more harm than good. Indeed a cynical philosopher has remarked that more harm is done in the world by the ignorant but well-meaning man than by the really wicked. If we do not wish to swell the ranks of the ignorant but well-meaning, we must set ourselves definitely to the acquisition of knowledge - knowledge which shall include the higher planes as well as the lower.

None can doubt that great forces of nature are playing in these realms of finer matter; and if any of them can be used by the unselfish man for the helping of his brother, then I say let us learn all that we can about these forces, whether they be mental, astral or physical. We know that knowledge enables us to give help to our fellows upon the physical plane, and we can see by analogy that if we are to be of use on the astral plane during sleep and after death, we certainly require knowledge there also. Let us then strive to gain such knowledge, and to gain it as soon and as fully as possible, so that no time may be wasted.

I do not for a moment seek to deny or to minimize the possible dangers of the astral plane. A man may misuse power upon any plane, and a man may be deceived upon any plane, and therefore on all planes alike he must be on his guard. In "The Voice of the Silence" we read, "Look not for thy Guru in these mâyâvic regions", and the caution is as urgently needed in these days as it could possibly have been in the days of Aryasangha. In Western countries at least there are hundreds of people who have accepted dead men as their teachers, each regarding the particular entity that communicates as a kind of private archangel specially sent by God to teach him or her. The Indian student ought not to need to be warned against such a mistake as this.

In the same book we are told that we must find our teacher on the mental plane - that his instruction must appeal to us through our intellect and not merely through our emotions. You may remember that one of your great Indian teachers, Siddhartha Gautama, whom men call the Buddha, especially cautioned his followers not to accept teaching which came to them by presumed spiritual inspiration, as from a deva - that is to say, not to accept it merely because it came in that way, but to judge it as all kinds of teaching must be judged - by the standard of one's own reason and one's own common sense. It is quite obvious that the dead man is not omniscient just because he happens to be dead; it is true that he has certain additional opportunities, but it by no means follows that he knows how to make use of them, and we must receive any statements that he makes with precisely the same reservations as we should have received statements made by him before he died.

If we adopt that method of testing everything by reason and by common sense we shall be quite safe in our efforts to understand the astral world. Remember that in that same book, "The Voice of the Silence", this astral world is spoken of as the 'Hall of Learning', showing that there is much valuable information to be acquired there by the student who approaches it wisely. If we thus keep the mind steady and the understanding clear, and if we test everything carefully as it comes to us, we shall never be drawn aside from the pursuit of the goal that lies before us by any temptation which the astral plane can offer. For those of us who are beginning to realize the existence and nature of the great divine scheme of evolution, the privilege of trying in our small way to help it forward is the one purpose of our existence. Of course it is true that that great scheme will be fulfilled whether we add to it our tiny mite of effort or not, yet it is unquestionably part of that scheme that those who have learned to understand it should co-operate intelligently in it, and that such effort is expected from us, and that its fulfillment will be hastened if we learn to throw our energies into it. We know that there will be those who will help; why should we not be among them? To us as to all is offered the opportunity of working as instruments in the hand of God; why should we not accept this opportunity? Since that glorious karma must come to some among men, let it be to us; why should we not be among those who share it? And yet, if we have really seen the glory of that scheme, it will be without any thought of karma that may accrue to us that we shall throw our whole hearts into the work; it will be simply because, having seen the grandeur and the beauty of the plan, there can be for us no other possibility than to devote the whole of our energies to trying to forward it. Let us then study any portion of that scheme which comes in our way, whether it be spiritual or mental, astral or physical, for all alike are parts of this great divine plan. Let us never for a moment lose sight of the goal which lies before us and of the spiritual development which is necessary for the attainment of that goal. But as long as we live in these lower planes, let us live well; and we can live well only if we live intelligently, and we can live intelligently only if we study the great laws of this universe of which we are a part.

What is the Tarot?

by P D. Ouspensky

No study of occult philosophy is possible without an acquaintance with symbolism, for if the words occultism and symbolism are correctly used, they mean almost one and the same thing. Symbolism cannot be learned as one learns to build bridges or speak a foreign language, and for the interpretation of symbols a special cast of mind is necessary; in addition to knowledge, special faculties, the power of creative thought and a developed imagination are required. One who understands the use of symbolism in the arts, knows, in a general way, what is meant by occult symbolism. But even then a special training of the mind is necessary, in order to comprehend the "language of the Initiates", and to express in this language the intuitions as they arise.

There are many methods for developing the "sense of symbols" in those who are striving to understand the hidden forces of Nature and Man, and for teaching the fundamental principles as well as the elements of the esoteric language. The most synthetic, and one of the most interesting of these methods, is the Tarot

In its exterior form the Tarot is a pack of cards used in the south of Europe for games and fortune-telling. These cards were first known in Europe at the end of the fourteenth century, when they were in use among the Spanish gypsies.

A pack of Tarot contains the fifty-two ordinary playing cards with the addition of one "picture card" to every suit, namely, the Knight, placed between the Queen and the Knave.

These fifty-six cards are divided into four suits, two black and two red and have the following designation: scepters (clubs), cups (hearts), swords (spades), and pentacles or disks (diamonds). In addition to the fifty-six cards the pack of Tarot has twenty-two numbered cards with special names:--

0 The Fool
1 The Magician.
2 The High Priestess.
3 The Empress.
4 The Emperor.
5 The Hierophant.
6 The Lovers.
7 The Chariot.
8 Strength.
9 The Hermit.
10 The Wheel of Fortune.
11 Justice.
12 The Hanged Man.
13 Death.
14 Temperance.
15 The Devil.
16 The Tower.
17 The Star.
18 The Moon.
19 The Sun.
20 Judgment.
21 The World.

This pack of cards, in the opinion of many investigators, represents the Egyptian hieroglyphic book of seventy-eight tablets, which came to us almost miraculously.

The history of the Tarot is a great puzzle. During the

Middle Ages, when it first appeared historically, there existed a tendency to build up synthetic symbolical or logical systems of the same sort as *Ars Magna* by Raymond Lully. But productions similar to the Tarot exist in India and China, so that we cannot possibly think it one of those systems created during the Middle Ages in Europe; it is also evidently connected with the Ancient Mysteries and the Egyptian Initiations. Although its origin is in oblivion and the aim of its author or authors quite unknown, there is no doubt whatever that it is the most complete code of Hermetic symbolism we possess.

Although represented as a pack of cards, the Tarot really is something quite different. It can be "read" in a variety of ways. As one instance, I shall give a metaphysical interpretation of the general meaning or of the general content of the book of Tarot, that is to say, its metaphysical title, which will plainly show that this work could not have been invented by illiterate gypsies of the fourteenth century.

The Tarot falls into three divisions: The first part has twenty-one numbered cards; the second part has one card 0; the third part has fifty-six cards, i. e., the four suits of fourteen cards. Moreover, the second part appears to be a link between the first and third parts, since all the fifty-six cards of the third part together are equal to the card 0.

Now, if we imagine twenty-one cards disposed in the shape of a triangle, seven cards on each side, a point in the center of the triangle represented by the zero card, and a square round the triangle (the square consisting of fifty-six cards, fourteen on each side), we shall have a representation of the relation between God, Man and the Universe, or the relation between the world of ideas, the consciousness of man and the physical world.

The triangle is God (the Trinity) or the world of ideas, or the noumenal world. The point is man's soul. The square is the visible, physical or phenomenal world. Potentially, the point is equal to the square, which means that all the visible world is contained in man's consciousness, is created in man's soul. And the soul itself is a point having no dimension in the world of the spirit, symbolized by the triangle. It is clear that such an idea could not have originated with ignorant people and clear also that the Tarot is something more than a pack of playing or fortune-telling cards.

H. P. Blavatsky mentions the Tarot in her works, and we have some reason for believing that she studied the Tarot. It is known that she loved to "play patience". We do not know what she read in the cards as she played this game, but the author was told that Madame Blavatsky searched persistently and for a long time for a MSS. on the Tarot.

In order to become acquainted with the Tarot, it is necessary to understand the basic ideas of the Kabala and of Alchemy. For it represents, as, indeed, many commentators of the Tarot think, a summary of the Hermetic Sciences--the Kabala, Alchemy, Astrology, Magic, with their different divisions. All these sciences, attributed to Hermes Trismegistus, really represent one system of a very broad and deep psychological investigation of the nature of man in his relation to the world of noumena (God, the world of Spirit) and to the world of phenomena (the visible, physical world). The letters of the Hebrew alphabet and the various allegories of the Kabala, the names of metals, acids and salts in alchemy; of planets and constellations in astrology; of good and evil spirits in magic--all these were only means to veil truth from the uninitiated.

But when the true alchemist spoke of seeking for gold, he spoke of gold in the soul of man. And he called gold that which in the New Testament is called the Kingdom of Heaven, and in Buddhism, Nirvana. And when the true astrologer spoke of constellations and planets he spoke of constellations and planets in the soul of man, i.e., of the qualities of the human soul and its relations to God and to the world. And when the true Kabalist spoke of the Name of God, he sought this Name in the soul of man and in Nature, not in dead books, nor in biblical texts, as did the Kabalist-Scholastics. The Kabala, Alchemy, Astrology, Magic are parallel symbolical systems of psychology and metaphysics. Any alchemical sentence may be read in a Kabalistic or astrological way, but the meaning will always be psychological and metaphysical.

We are surrounded by a wall built of our conceptions of the world, and are unable to look over this wall at the real world. The Kabala presents an effort to break this "enchanted circle". It investigates the world as it is, the world in itself.

The world in itself, as the Kabalists hold, consists of four elements, or the four principles forming One. These four principles are represented by the four letters of the name of Jehovah. The basic idea of the Kabala consists in the study of the Name of God in its manifestation. Jehovah in Hebrew is spelt by four letters, Yod, He, Vau and He--I. H. V. H. To these four letters is given the deepest symbolical meaning. The first letter expresses the active principle, the beginning or first cause, motion, energy, "I"; the second letter expresses the passive element, inertia, quietude, "not I;" the third, the balance of opposites, "form"; and the fourth, the result or latent energy.

The Kabalists affirm that every phenomenon and every

object consists of these four principles, i.e., that every object and every phenomenon consists of the Name of God (The Word),--Logos.

The study of this Name (or the four-lettered word, Tetragrammaton, in Greek) and the finding of it in everything constitutes the main problem of Kabalistic philosophy.

To state it in another way the Kabalists hold that these four principles penetrate and create everything. Therefore, when the man finds these four principles in things and phenomena of quite different categories (where before he had not seen similarity), he begins to see analogy between these phenomena. And, gradually, he becomes convinced that the whole world is built according to one and the same law, on one and the same plan. The richness and growth of his intellect consists in the widening of his faculty for finding analogies. Therefore the study of the law of the four letters, or the name of Jehovah presents a powerful means for widening consciousness.

This idea is perfectly clear, for if the Name of God be really in all (if God be present in all), all should be analogous to each other--the smallest particle analogous to the whole, the speck of dust analogous to the universe, and all analogous to God. The Name of God, the Word or Logos is the origin of the world. Logos also means Reason; the Word is the Logos, the Reason of everything.

There is a complete correspondence between the Kabala and Alchemy and Magic. In Alchemy the four elements, which constitute the real world are called fire, water, air and earth; these fully correspond in significance with the four kabalistic letters. In Magic they are expressed as the four classes of spirits:

elves (or salamanders), undines, sylphs and gnomes.

The Tarot in its turn is quite analogous to the Kabala, Alchemy and Magic, and, as it were, includes them. Corresponding to the four first principles or four letters of the Name of God, or the four alchemistic elements, or the four classes of spirits, the Tarot has four suits--scepters, cups, swords and pentacles. Thus every suit, every side of the square, equal to the point, represents one of the elements, controls one class of spirits. The scepters are fire or elves (or salamanders); the cups are water or undines; the swords are air or sylphs; and pentacles, earth or gnomes. Moreover, in every suit the King means the first principle or fire; the Queen--the second principle or water; the Knight--the third principle or air, and the Page (knave)--the fourth principle or earth.

Then again, the ace means fire; the deuce water; the three-spot, air; the four-spot earth. Then again the four-spot is the first principle, the five spot, the second etc.

In regard to the suits, one may add that the black suits (scepters and swords) express activity and energy, will, initiative and the subjective side of consciousness; and the red (cups and pentacles) express passivity, inertia and the objective side of consciousness. Then the first two suits (scepters and cups) signify "good" and the other two (swords and pentacles) mean "evil". Thus every card of the fifty-six indicates (independently of its number) the presence of the principle of activity or passivity, of "good" or "evil", arising either in man's will or from without. And the significance of each card is further deciphered thorough its various combinations with the suits and numbers in their symbolical meaning. The fifty-six cards as a whole represent, as it were, a complete picture of all the possibilities of man's consciousness. And this makes the Tarot adaptable for fortune-telling. Thus, including the Kabala, Astrology, Alchemy and Magic, the Tarot makes it possible to "seek gold", "to evoke spirits," and "to draw horoscopes", simply by means of this pack of cards without the complicated paraphernalia and ceremonies of an alchemist, astrologer or magician.

But the main interest of Tarot is in the twenty-two numbered cards. These cards have numerical meaning and also a very involved symbolical significance.

The literature relating to the Tarot has in view mainly the reading of the symbolical designs of the twenty-two cards. Very many writers on occultism have arranged their works on the plan of the Tarot. But this is not often suspected because the Tarot is rarely mentioned. Oswald Wirth speaks of origin of the Tarot in his Essay upon the Astronomical Tarot.

"According to Christian in his *Histoire de la Magie*, the twenty-two major arcana of the Tarot represent the hieroglyphic paintings which were found in the spaces between the columns of a gallery which the neophyte was obliged to cross in the Egyptian initiations. There were twelve columns to the north and the same number to the south, that is, eleven symbolical pictures on each side. These pictures were explained to the candidate for initiation in regular order, and they contained the rules and principles for the Initiate. This opinion is confirmed by the correspondence which exists between arcana when they are thus arranged."

In the gallery of the Temple the pictures were arranged in pairs, one opposite another, so that the last picture was opposite the first, the last but one opposite the second, etc.

When the cards are so placed we find a highly interesting and deep suggestion. In this way the mind finds the one in the two, and is led from dualism to monism, which is what we might call the unification of the duad. One card explains the other and each pair shows moreover that they can be only mutually explanatory and mean nothing when taken separately.

Thus, for instance, the cards 10 and 13 ("Life" and "Death") signify together a certain whole or complementary condition which we cannot conceive by the ordinary, imperfect mental processes. We think of life and death as two "opposites", antagonistic one to the other, but, if we thought further, we should see that each depends on the other for existence and neither could come into existence separately.

A symbol may serve to transfer our intuitions and to suggest new ones only so long as its meaning is not defined. Real symbols are perpetually in process of creation; but when they receive a definite significance they become hieroglyphs and finally a mere alphabet. As this they express simply ordinary concepts, cease to be a language of the Gods or of initiates and become a language of men which everyone may learn.

Properly speaking, a symbol in occultism means the same as in art. If an artist uses ready-made symbols his work will not be true art, but only pseudo-art,. If an occultist begins to use ready-made symbols, his work will not be truly occult, for it will contain no esotericism, no mysticism, but only pseudo-occultism, pseudo-esotericism, pseudo-mysticism. Symbolism in which the symbols have definite meanings is pseudo-symbolism.

Having made this idea clear in his mind, the author

found that the key to the Tarot must lie in imagination and he decided to make an effort to re-design the cards, giving descriptive pictures of the Tarot, and to interpret the symbols, not by means of analysis, but by synthesis. The reader will find in the following little "pen pictures" reflections of many authors who wrote on the Tarot as St. Martin, Eliphas Levi, Dr. Papus etc. and of other authors who certainly never thought of the Tarot as, for example, Plotinus, Gichtel, Friedrich Nietzsche, M. Collins etc., who came nevertheless to the same fundamental principles as the unknown authors of the Tarot.

Descriptions of the arcanas in these "pen pictures" often represent a conception which is almost entirely subjective, for instance, that of card 18. And the author likes to think that another might conceive of the same symbols differently, in any case he considers this quite possible.

Anyone interested in this philosophical puzzle might well ask, What then is the Tarot? Is it a doctrine or merely a method? Is it a definite system or merely an alphabet by means of which any system may be constructed? In short, is it a book containing specific teachings, or is it merely an apparatus, a machine which we may use to build anything, even a new universe.

The author believes that the Tarot may be used for both purposes, though, of course, the contents of a book that may be read either forward or backward cannot be said to be, in the ordinary sense, strictly definite. But perhaps we find in this very indefiniteness of the Tarot and in the complexity of its philosophy, the element which constitutes its definiteness. The fact that we question the Tarot as to whether it be a method or a doctrine shows the limitation of our "three dimensional mind," which is unable to rise above the world of form and contra-positions or to free itself from thesis and antithesis! Yes, the Tarot contains and expresses any doctrine to be found in our consciousness, and in this sense it has definiteness. It represents Nature in all the richness of its infinite possibilities, and there is in it as in Nature, not one but all potential meanings. And these meanings are fluent and ever-changing, so the Tarot cannot be specifically this or that, for it ever moves and yet is ever the same.

The Importance of Ceremonial Magic

by Arthur Edward Waite

The ordinary fields of psychological inquiry, largely in possession of the pathologist, are fringed by a borderland of occult and dubious experiment into which pathologists may occasionally venture, but it is left for the most part to unchartered explorers. Beyond these fields and this borderland there lies the legendary wonder-world of Theurgy, so called, of Magic and Sorcery, a world of fascination or terror, as the mind which regards it is tempered, but in either case the antithesis of admitted possibility. There all paradoxes seem to obtain actually, contradictions coexist logically, the effect is greater than the cause and the shadow more than the substance. Therein the visible melts into the unseen, the invisible is manifested openly, motion from place to place is accomplished without traversing the intervening distance, matter passes through matter. There two straight lines may enclose a space; space has a fourth dimension, and untrodden fields beyond it; without metaphor and without evasion, the circle is mathematically squared. There life is prolonged, youth renewed, physical immortality secured. There earth becomes gold, and gold earth. There words and wishes possess creative power, thoughts are things, desire realizes its object. There, also, the dead live and the hierarchies of extra-mundane intelligence are within easy communication, and become ministers or tormentors, guides or destroyers, of man. There the Law of Continuity is suspended by the interference of the higher Law of Fantasia.

But, unhappily, this domain of enchantment is in all respects comparable to the gold of Faerie, which is presumably its medium of exchange. It cannot withstand daylight, the test of the human eye, or the scale of reason. When these are applied, its paradox becomes an anticlimax, its antithesis ludicrous; its contradictions are without genius; its mathematical marvels end in a verbal quibble; its elixirs fail even as purges; its transmutations do not need exposure at the assayer's hands; its marvel-working words prove barbarous mutilations of dead languages, and are impotent from the moment that they are understood; departed friends, and even planetary intelligences, must not be seized by the skirts, for they are apt to desert their draperies, and these are not like the mantle of Elijah.

The little contrast here instituted will serve to exhibit that there are at least two points of view regarding Magic and its mysteries--the simple and homogeneous view, prevailing within a charmed circle among the few survivals whom reason has not hindered from entering, and that of the world without, which is more complex, more composite, but sometimes more reasonable only by imputation. There is also a third view, in which legend is checked by legend and wonder substituted for wonder. Here it is not the Law of Continuity persisting in its formulae despite the Law of Fantasia; it is Croquemetaine explained by Diabolus, the runes of Elf-land read with the interpretation of Infernus; it is the Law of Bell and Candle, the Law of Exorcism, and its final expression is in the terms of the *auto-da-fé*. For this view the wonder-world exists without any question, except that of the Holy Tribunal; it is not what it seems, but is adjustable to the eye of faith in the light from the Lamp of the Sanctuaries; in a word, its angels are demons, its Melusines stryges, its phantoms vampires, its spells and mysteries the Black Science. Here Magic itself rises up and responds that there is a Black and a White Art, an Art of Hermes and an Art of Canidia, a Science of the Height and a

Science of the Abyss, of Metatron and Belial. In this manner a fourth point of view emerges; they are all, however, illusive; there is the positive illusion of the legend, affirmed by the remaining adherents of its literal sense, and the negative illusion which denies the legend crassly without considering that there is a possibility behind it; there is the illusion which accounts for the legend by an opposite hypothesis, and the illusion of the legend which reaffirms itself with a distinction. When these have been disposed of, there remain two really important questions--the question of the Mystics and the question of history and literature. To a very large extent the first is closed to discussion, because the considerations which it involves cannot be presented with profit on either side in the public assemblies of the reading world. So far as may be held possible, it has been dealt with already. As regards the second, it is the large concern and purpose of this inquiry, and the limits of its importance may therefore be stated shortly.

There can be no extensive literatures without motives proportionate to account for them. If we take the magical literature of Western Europe from the Middle Ages and onward, we shall find that it is moderately large. Now, the acting principles in the creation of that literature will prove to rule also in its history; what is obscure in the one may be understood by help of the other; each reacted upon each; as the literature grew, it helped to make the history, and the new history was so much additional material for further literature.

There were, of course, many motive principles at work, for the literature and history of Magic are alike exceedingly intricate, and there are many interpretations of principles which are apt to be confused with the principles, as, for example, the influence of what is loosely called superstition upon ignorance; these and any interpretations must be ruled out of an inquiry like the present. The main principles are summed in the conception of a number of assumed mysterious forces in the universe which could be put in operation by man, or at least followed in their secret processes. In the ultimate, however, they could all be rendered secondary, if not passive, to the will of man; for even in astrology, which was the discernment of forces regarded as peculiarly fatal, there was an art of ruling, and *sapiens dominabitur astris* became an axiom of the science. This conception culminated or centered in the doctrine of unseen, intelligent powers, with whom it was possible for prepared persons to communicate; the methods by which this communication was attempted are the most important processes of Magic, and the books which embody these methods, called Ceremonial Magic, are the most important part of the literature. Here, that is to say, is the only branch of the subject which it is necessary to understand in order to understand the history. Had Magic been focused in the reading of the stars, it would have possessed no history to speak of, for astrology involved intellectual equipments which, comparatively speaking, were possible only to the few. Had Magic centered in the transmutation of metals, it would never have moved multitudes, but would have remained what that still is, the quixotic hope which emerges at a far distance from the science of chemistry. We may take the remaining occult sciences collectively, but there is nothing in them of themselves which would make history. In virtue of the synthetic doctrine which has been already formulated, they were all magically possible, but they were all subsidiary to that which was head and crown of all--the art of dealing with spirits. The presumed possession of the secret of this art made Magic formidable, and made therefore its history. There was a time indeed when Ceremonial Magic threatened to absorb the whole circle of the occult sciences; it was the superior method, the royal road; it effected immediately what the others accomplished laboriously, after a long time. It had, moreover, the palmary recommendation that it was a conventional art, working by definite formula; above all, it was a process in words.

It was the fascination of this process which brought men and women-all sorts and conditions of both--to the Black Sabbath and to the White Sabbath, and blinded them to the danger of the stake. It was the full and clear acceptance of this process as effectual by Church and State which kindled the faggots for the magician in every Christian land. Astrology was scarcely discouraged, and if the alchemist were occasionally tortured, it was only to extract his secret. There was no danger in these things, and hence there was no judgment against them, except by imputation from their company; but Magic, but dealing with spirits, was that which made even the peasant tremble, and when the peasant shakes at his hearth, the king is not secure in his palace nor the Pope at St. Peter's, unless both can protect their own. Moreover, in the very claim of Ceremonial Magic there was an implied competition with the essential claim of the Church.

The importance of Ceremonial Magic, and of the literature which embodies it, to the history of the occult sciences being admitted, there is no need to argue that this history is a legitimate and reasonable study; in such a case, knowledge is its own end, and there can be certainly no question as to the distinguished influence which has been exercised by the belief in Magic throughout the ages. In order, however, to understand the literature of Magic, it is necessary to obtain first of all a clear principle of regarding it. It will be superfluous to say that we must surrender the legends, as such, to those who work in legends, and dispute about their essential value. We need not debate whether Magic, for example, can really square the circle, as magicians testify, or whether such an operation is impossible even to Magic, as commonly would be objected by those who deny the art. We need not seriously discuss the proposition that the devil assists the magicians to perform a mathematical impossibility, or its qualified form, that the circle can be squared indifferently by those who invoke the angel Cassiel of the hierarchy of Uriel and those who invoke Astaroth. We shall see very shortly, as already indicated, that we are dealing with a bizarre literature, which passes, by various fantastic phases, through all folly into crime. We have to account for these characteristics.

The desire to communicate with spirits is older than history; it connects with ineradicable principles in human nature, which have been discussed too often for it to be necessary to recite them here; and the attempts to satisfy that desire have usually taken a shape which does gross outrage to reason. Between the most ancient processes, such as those of Chaldean Magic, and the rites of the Middle Ages, there are marked correspondences, and there is something of common doctrine, as distinct from intention, in which identity would more or less obtain, underlying them both. The doctrine of compulsion, or the power which both forms pretended to exercise even upon superior spirits by the use of certain words, is a case in point. In approaching the Ceremonial Magic of the Middle Ages, we must therefore bear in mind that we are dealing with a literature which, though modern in its actual presentation, embodies some elements of great antiquity. It is doubtful whether the presence of these elements can be accounted for on the principle that mankind in all ages works unconsciously for the accomplishment of similar intentions in an analogous way; a bizarre intention, of course, tends independently to be fulfilled in a bizarre manner, but in this case the similarity is so close that it is more easily explained by the perpetuation--sporadic and natural or concerted and artificial--of an antique tradition, for which channels could be readily assigned. There is one upon the face of the literature, and that is the vehicle of Kabalistic symbolism, though it cannot be held to cover the entire distance in time.

There have been two ways of regarding the large and imperfectly explored literature which embodies the Kabalah of the Jews, and these in turn will give two methods of accounting for the spurious and grotesque processes which enter so extensively into Ceremonial Magic. It is treated either as a barren mystification, a collection of supremely absurd treatises, in which obscure nonsense is enunciated with preternatural solemnity, or it is regarded as a body of theosophy, written chiefly in the form of symbolism. The first view is that which is formed, I suppose, almost irresistibly upon a superficial acquaintance, and there is not any need to add that it is the one which obtains generally in derived judgments, for here, as in other cases, the second-hand opinion issues from the most available source. It is just to add that it does not differ very seriously from the opinions expressed in the past by a certain section of scholarship. The alternative judgment is that which prevails among those students of the literature who have approached it with a certain preparation through acquaintance with other channels of the Secret Tradition. From the one it would follow that the Ceremonial Magic which at a long distance draws from the Kabalah, reproduces its absurdities, possibly with further exaggerations, or it is the subject-matter of the literature carried to its final results. Two erroneous views have issued from the other--an exaggerated importance attributed to the processes in question on the ground of their exalted connections, and--this, however, is rarely met with--an inclination to regard them also as symbolical writing.

There is no ground for the criticism of the first

inference, which has arisen legitimately enough and is that which will be most acceptable to the majority of readers. Those who value Kabalistic literature as a storehouse of symbolism, the inner sense of which is or may be of importance, but see nothing in the processes of Ceremonial Magic to make them momentous in their literal sense or susceptible to interpretation, will be tempted to dismiss them as medieval and later impostures, which must be carefully distinguished from the true symbolical tradition. In either case the ceremonial literature is disdainfully rejected, and it follows in this manner that alternatives which exclude one another both reach the truth as their term.

There is, however, yet another point of view, and it is of some moment, as it connects with that question of the Instituted Mysteries about which it has been already observed that very little has transpired. Most students of occultism are acquainted with intimations and rumors of the existence in modern times of more than one Occult as of more than one Mystical Fraternity, deriving, or believed to derive, from other associations of the past. There are, of course, many unaffiliated occultists, as most mystics are unaffiliated, but the secret Fraternities exist, and the keys of occult symbolism are said to be in their possession. From a variety of isolated statements scattered up and down the works of professed Occultists in recent years, it is possible to summarize broadly the imputed standpoint of these bodies in respect of Ceremonial Magic. I will express it in brief as follows. There is no extant Ritual, as there is no doctrine, which contains, or can possibly contain, the real secret of magical procedure or the essence of occult doctrine. The reason--whatever may be said in the excess of some self-constituted exponents--is not because there is, or can be, any indicible process, but because the knowledge in question is in the custody of those who have taken effectual measures for its protection; and though, from time to time, some secrets of initiation, belonging to this order, have filtered through printed books into the world at large, the real mysteries have never escaped. The literature of Magic falls, therefore, on this hypothesis, under three heads: (*a.*) The work of putative adepts, stating as much as could be stated outside the circle of initiation, and primarily designed to attract those who might be ripe for entrance. (*b.*) The speculations of independent seekers, who, by thought, study and intuition, sometimes attained veridic results without assistance. (*c.*) Travesties of occult doctrine, travesties of occult intention, travesties of occult procedure, complicated by filtrations from the superior source.

The opinions of professed occultists on any subject whatsoever are of no importance to myself, and are named only to establish a point of view; but most Ceremonial Magic belongs to the third class, on the assumption that it still exists, like some other paths of Satanism; the first, by its nature, is not represented, and the second only slightly. In a word, Ceremonial Magic reflects mainly the egregious ambitions and incorporates the mad processes of medieval sorcery--of the Sabbath above all. The additional elements are debased applications of various Kabalistic methods, seering processes current among country people and fantastic attempts to reduce magical legends to a formal practice.

Whichever of the above views the reader may prefer to adopt, it will be seen that the net result as regards the Rituals is not generically different, that they are of literary and historical interest, but nothing further. For the occultist they will possess, from their associations, an importance which will be of no moment to another student. It is desirable that they should not be undervalued, as records of the past, because they have exercised an influence, and they are memorable as curiosities thereof; but it is more desirable still that the weak and credulous should be warned against acting like fools, and that those who are seeking spiritual certitude should be dissuaded from the science of the abyss.

The Golden Verses of Pythagoras

attributed to Pythagoras

1. First worship the Immortal Gods, as they are established and ordained by the Law.

2. Reverence the Oath, and next the Heroes, full of goodness and light.

3. Honor likewise the Terrestrial Dæmons by rendering them the worship lawfully due to them.

4. Honor likewise thy parents, and those most nearly related to thee.

5. Of all the rest of mankind, make him thy friend who distinguishes himself by his virtue.

6. Always give ear to his mild exhortations, and take example from his virtuous and useful actions.

7. Avoid as much as possible hating thy friend for a slight fault.

8. And understand that power is a near neighbor to necessity.

9. Know that all these things are as I have told thee; and accustom thyself to overcome and vanquish these passions:

10. First gluttony, sloth, sensuality, and anger.

11. Do nothing evil, neither in the presence of others, nor privately;

12. But above all things respect thyself.

13. In the next place, observe justice in thy actions and in thy words.

14. And accustom not thyself to behave thyself in any thing without rule, and without reason.

15. But always make this reflection, that it is ordained by destiny that all men shall die.

16. And that the goods of fortune are uncertain; and that as they may be acquired, so may they likewise be lost.

17. Concerning all the calamities that men suffer by divine fortune,

18. Support with patience thy lot, be it what it may, and never repine at it.

19. But endeavor what thou canst to remedy it.

20. And consider that fate does not send the greatest portion of these misfortunes to good men.

21. There are among men many sorts of reasonings, good and bad;

22. Admire them not too easily, nor reject them.

23. But if falsehoods be advanced, hear them with mildness, and arm thyself with patience.

24. Observe well, on every occasion, what I am going to tell thee:

25. Let no man either by his words, or by his deeds, ever seduce thee.

26. Nor entice thee to say or to do what is not profitable for thyself.

27. Consult and deliberate before thou act, that thou mayest not commit foolish actions.

28. For it is the part of a miserable man to speak and to act without reflection.

29. But do that which will not afflict thee afterwards, nor oblige thee to repentance.

30. Never do anything which thou dost not understand.

31. But learn all thou ought'st to know, and by that means thou wilt lead a very pleasant life.

32. In no wise neglect the health of thy body;

33. But give it drink and meat in due measure, and also the exercise of which it has need.

34. Now by measure I mean what will not incommode thee.

35. Accustom thyself to a way of living that is neat and decent without luxury.

36. Avoid all things that will occasion envy.

37. And be not prodigal out of season, like one who knows not what is decent and honorable.

38. Neither be covetous nor miserly; a due measure is excellent in these things.

39. Do only the things that cannot hurt thee, and deliberate before thou dost them.

40. Never suffer sleep to close thy eyelids, after thy going to bed,

41. Till thou hast examined by thy reason all thy actions of the day.

42. Wherein have I done amiss? What have I done? What have I omitted that I ought to have done?

43. If in this examination thou find that thou hast done amiss, reprimand thyself severely for it;

44. And if thou hast done any good, rejoice.

45. Practice thoroughly all these things; meditate on them well; thou oughtest to love them with all thy heart.

46. 'Tis they that will put thee in the way of divine virtue.

47. I swear it by him who has transmitted into our souls the Sacred Quaternion, the source of nature, whose cause is eternal.

48. But never begin to set thy hand to any work, till thou hast first prayed to the gods to accomplish what thou art going to begin.

49. When thou hast made this habit familiar to thee,

50. Thou wilt know the constitution of the Immortal Gods

and of men.

51. Even how far the different beings extend, and what contains and binds them together.

52. Thou shalt likewise know that according to Law, the nature of this universe is in all things alike,

53. So that thou shalt not hope what thou ought'st not to hope; and nothing in this world shall be hid from thee.

54. Thou wilt likewise know, that men draw upon themselves their own misfortunes voluntarily, and of their own free choice.

55. Unhappy that they are! They neither see nor understand that their good is near them.

56. Few know how to deliver themselves out of their misfortunes.

57. Such is the fate that blinds mankind, and takes away his senses.

58. Like huge cylinders they roll to and fro, and always oppressed with ills innumerable.

59. For fatal strife, innate, pursues them everywhere, tossing them up and down; nor do they perceive it.

60. Instead of provoking and stirring it up, they ought, by yielding, to avoid it.

61. Oh! Jupiter, our Father! if Thou would'st deliver men from all the evils that oppress them,

62. Show them of what dæmon they make use.

63. But take courage; the race of man is divine.

64. Sacred nature reveals to them the most hidden mysteries.

65. If she impart to thee her secrets, thou wilt easily perform all the things which I have ordained thee.

66. And by the healing of thy soul, thou wilt deliver it from all evils, from all afflictions.

67. But abstain thou from the meats, which we have forbidden in the purifications and in the deliverance of the soul;

68. Make a just distinction of them, and examine all things well.

69. Leaving thyself always to be guided and directed by the understanding that comes from above, and that ought to hold the reins.

70. And when, after having divested thyself of thy mortal body, thou arrivest at the most pure Æther,

71. Thou shalt be a God, immortal, incorruptible, and Death shall have no more dominion over thee.

The Legend of the Holy Grail and its Connection with Templars and Freemasons

by Arthur Edward Waite

Part I

Sketch of the Connection

If deeper pitfalls are laid by anything more than by the facts of coincidence, it is perhaps by the intimations and suggestions of writings which bear the stamp of allegory or concealed allusion on their surface; as in the cases of coincidence, so in these it is necessary for the historical critic to be very much upon his guard, and not to accept correspondences, however plausible, unless they are controlled and strengthened by more substantial evidence.

But the fact of the correspondences remains; they are important within their own sphere; and it is often through indirect lights of this kind that research has been led into new tracks from which unexpected and indubitable results have ultimately followed. It is the purpose of the present paper to indicate certain analogies which are at least curious and to stimulate further investigation along the lines which they appear to indicate, without attempting at the moment to press any definite conclusion.

Some slight general acquaintance with the Legend of the Holy Grail may for the moment be presupposed in the reader, though the legend itself will be made quite clear as we proceed. It is proposed for the first time in the history of the subject to institute a connection between the knightly quest of the Grail, as undertaken by the chivalry of King Arthur's Court, and the allegorical quest which is undertaken in Freemasonry, as the candidate progresses from grade to grade. The connecting link between the two things, to all appearance so widely divergent, must be sought outside of each, and it is found in the Ancient Order of the Knights Templar who, according to a well-known, though by no means universally accepted view, are the ancestors of the modern Freemason, and, as it will be sought to show, were possibly the originators or conservers of the Grail legend. If such a view should prove to be well-founded, two things will follow of necessity: (1) modern archaeology will have to revise its notions on the subject of the Grail in medieval and romantic literature; and (2) the history of Masonry will require to be rewritten. This statement summarizes in a few words an enormous complexity of issues to which no justice can be done in what must at best be only a preliminary sketch. As much archeological or masonic knowledge must not be assumed in the reader, it may be premised further that he will acquire without difficulty as he proceeds the little that is essential for a proper understanding of the subject. It is not necessary that he should be either a literary scholar familiar with the byways of the mediaeval romances, and with their criticism, or, on the other hand, that he should he himself a member of the masonic fraternity. Attendance will be asked in the first place to the following points, which will simplify the later considerations.

There are at the present time two schools of masonic criticism with regard to the origin of the fraternity. For the one it is the natural descendant of the old building guilds or trade unions of the past, which from a remote period were in the habit of admitting into their ranks influential persons who were neither architects nor builders. At a certain epoch of time, which it is difficult to indicate, except within rather broad limits, but with England as its locality, some of these lay members would appear to have found themselves practically in possession of certain lodges, and they converted the old mystery or mummery of masonry into an allegorical or speculative system applied to the morals of its professors, which new system so spread that it absorbed or ousted the original trading element and laid the ground-work of that vast confederation which at this day covers the whole earth. This, somewhat roughly indicated, is the accepted view, the view taken by the major part of the educated opinion within the ranks of the fraternity, because it tends to minimize the element of mystery and wonder which is inseparable from subjects of the kind by exhibiting things which are unknown or dubious in the aspect of things familiar. By the other school it is believed that at the suppression of the Templars by King Philippe le Bel and Pope Clement in 1307, that knightly order did not in reality, or at least utterly perish, but assumed the disguise of freemasonry, taking refuge in certain lodges of the building guilds, and importing into these the secret speculative and religious doctrine which it had learned in the east, and on account of which the Pope and King combined in the attempt to destroy it. This view finds expression more particularly in France and Germany, but it has had its exponents in England; it has rested so far on insufficient foundations from the standpoint of historical evidence, but it represents a tradition which it is difficult to ignore with justice and entirely, and it is possible that it may yet receive unexpected substantiation. It will be obvious that one important step in this direction will be made by establishing an analogy between masonic symbolism and that of the Grail legend, the Templar connections of which have been put forward successfully by scholars, both in England and Germany, whose decision, if not final, is at least entitled to the very highest respect. The connections, moreover, as will be seen, appear on the face of the legend in some of its most important forms.

With a view to the simplification of an inquiry which touches upon several fields of research which are all of them highly specialized, the first consideration will be given to the Legend of the Holy Grail and its sources in medieval literature; the traces of Templarism therein will be dealt with in the next place, together with a short account of what has been surmised concerning the secret doctrine of the Templars and the alleged survival of the Order; the connection of both with the chief legend of Masonry will be shown in the last place, and a tentative inference will be attempted.

The Legend of the Holy Grail and its Connection with Templars and Freemasons

Part II

Some Aspects of the Grail Legend

There are a few legends which may be said to stand forth among the innumerable traditions of humanity, wearing upon them the external signs or characters of some secret or mystery within them which seems to belong rather to eternity than to time. They are, in no sense, connected with one another, and yet, by a suggestion which is deeper than any suggestion of the senses, they would seem as if each of them were appealing to each, one bearing testimony to another and all recalling all. They might be the broken fragments of a primitive revelation which, except in these memorials, has passed out of time and mind. There are also other legends, strange, melancholy and long haunting, which seem to have issued from the depths of aboriginal humanity, below all horizons of history, pointing to terrible periods of a past which is of the body only and not of the soul of man, and hinting that, once upon a time, there was a soulless age of our race, when minds were formless as the mammoths of geological epochs. To the latter class belongs some of what remains to us of the folklore of the cave-dwellers, the traditions of the pre-Ayran races of Europe. To the former, among many others, belongs the Grail Legend which, at least in its purest aspects, is to be classed among the legends of the soul.

It might seem at first sight almost a superfluous precaution, even in an elementary paper, to give an answer to the question, What, then, was the Holy Grail? Those who are unacquainted with its literature in the old books of chivalry, by which it first entered into the romance of Europe, will know it by the "Idylls of the King." But it is not so superfluous as it seems, and many answers to the question have been attempted which are altogether different from that which is given by the knight Percival to his fellow monk in the poem of Tennyson.

> *"What Is it? The phantom of a cup that comes and goes?"*
>
> *"Nay, monk! what phantom?" answer'd Percivale.*
> *"The cup, the cup itself, from which our Lord*
> *Drank at the last sad supper with his own.*
> *This, from the blessed land of Aromat...*
> *Arimathsean Joseph, journeying brought*
> *To Glastonbury...*
>
> *And thus a while It bode; and if a man*
> *Could touch or see It, he was heal'd at once*
> *By faith of all his Ills; But then the times*
> *Grew to such evil that the Holy Cup*
> *Was caught away to Heaven and disappear'd."*

That is the answer with which in one or another of is forms, poetic or chivalrous, everyone is expected to be acquainted, or must be classed as too unlettered for consideration, even in a slight sketch of the present kind. But, as hinted already, it is so little the only answer, and it so little full or exhaustive, that no person acquainted with the literature would accept it otherwise than as one of its aspects, and even the enchanting gift of the laureate's poetic faculty leaves- and that of necessity- something to be desired in the summary of the knight's reply to the direct question of the monk Ambrosius. There is an allusiveness, a pregnancy, a suggestion about the legend in its best forms which escapes in such an answer; it is found in the old romances, especially in the romantic chronicle of Sir Percival and the "Morte d'Arthur." It is found later on in Tennyson's own poem, when Percival's sister, the nun of "utter whiteness," describes her vision :—

> *"I heard a sound*
> *As of a silver horn from o'er the hills. . . .*
>
> *the slender sound*
> *As from a distance beyond distance grew*
> *Coming upon me. .*
>
> *and then*
> *Stream'd thro' my cell a cold and silver beam*
> *And down the long beam stole the Holy Grail.*
> *Rose-red with beatings in it."*
>
> And again:—
> *"I saw the spiritual city and all her spires*
> *And gateways in a glory like one ear . . . .*
> *Strike from the sea and from the star there shot*
> *A rose-red sparkle to the city, and there*
> *Dwelt, and I knew it was the Holy Grail."*

So also in the chivalric books the legend is treated with an aloofness, and yet with a directness of circumstance and a manifoldness of detail awakening a sense of reality amidst enchantment which is scarcely heightened when the makers of the old chronicles testify to the truth of their story. The explanation is, according to one version of the Quest, that it was written by Christ himself after the Resurrection, and that there is no clerk, "however hardy," who will dare to suggest that any other scripture is referable to the same hand. Sir Thomas Malory, the latest and best of the compilers of the Arthurian legend, suppresses this ascription, and in the colophon of his eighteenth book is contented with adding that it is "a story chronicled for one of the truest and holiest that is in this world."

But there is ample evidence in Sir Thomas Malory's own book, the "Morte d'Arthur," that the Grail L end was derived into his great chronicle from various sources, and that several elements entered into it which are quite excluded by the description of Sir Percival in the "Idylls," or by the colophon of his own twelfth book, which reads: *"And here followeth the noble tale of the Sancgreal that called is the hooly vessel, and the sygnefycacyon of blessid blood of our Lord Jhesu Cryste, blessid mote it be, the whiche was brought into this land by Joseph of Armathye, therefore on all synful souls Blessid Lord have Thou mercy."*

It is not necessary, or indeed possible, to particularize all these elements, but, as an equipoise to the religious or sacramental side of the legend, it has been pointed out that the French romance, from which the English version is chiefly derived, would appear to have borrowed from old Irish stories of the pagan period something concerning a mysterious magical vessel full of miraculous food. This is illustrated by the "Morte d'Arthur" in the memorable episode of the high festival held by King Arthur at Pentecost. "In the midst of the supper there entered into the hall the Holy Grail covered with white Samite, but there was none might see it or who bore it, and then was all the hall fulfilled with good odors and every knight had such meats and drinks as he best loved in this world." That is a state of the legend which has little connection with the mystic vessel carried out of Palestine by the centurion of the evangelists, but the simple minded chroniclers of the past did not observe the anachronism when they married the Christian fable to any parallel history which came in their way.

The Legend of the Holy Grail and its Connection with Templars and Freemasons

Part III
Epochs of the Legend

A minute enquiry into the materials and their sources of a moving and stately legend are opposed to the purposes and interests of the general reader, for whom the Grail has two epochs only in literature, that of Sir Thomas Malory and that of "The Idylls of the King," and as Tennyson was indebted to Malory, so it is through his gracious poems that most persons have been sent back to the old book of chivalry from which he reproduced his motives and sometimes derived his words. But without entering into the domain of archaeology, the lettered student, and, indeed, the literate reader, will know well enough that there are branches of the legend outside these two great names, and that some of them are close enough to his hand. He will know that the Cornish poet, Robert Stephen Hawker's "Quest of the San Grail" has, as Madame de Stael once said of Saint Martin, "some sublime gleams." He will know that the old French romance of Percival le Gallois recently translated into English of an archaic kind by Dr. Sebastian Evans, is a gorgeous romance, full of richly painted pictures and endless pageants. He will know finally that there is a German cycle of the Grail traditions, and that Titurel, Parsifal and Lohengrin, to whom a strange and wonderful life beyond all common teachings of nature, and beyond all common conventions of art has been given by Wagner, are also legendary heroes of the Holy Grail. There are, therefore, broadly speaking, three points of view as regards this subject, which are—

(1) The Romantic ; and the reversion of literary

sentiment at the present day towards romanticism will make it unnecessary to say that this is now a very strong point. It is exemplified by the numerous editions of the "Morte d'Arthur," produced not only for students, but also in the interests of children, and in which a large space is invariably given to the Grail Legend. Lang's "Book of Romance" and Mary McCleod's "Book of King Arthur and His Noble Knights," are instances which will occur to most people; but there are many others.

(2) The Poetic, to which, having regard to what has been said already, it is only necessary to add that it has done something to exalt and spiritualize the legend without removing the romantic element. In the case of Tennyson it has certainly added the elevated emotion which belongs essentially to the spirit of romance, and has saved English literature during the latter half of the 19th century. But taking the work at its highest, it may well be that the Grail Legend has still to receive its treatment more fully by some poet who is to come. The literary form of this particular Idyll of the King, a tale within a tale twice told, leaves something to be desired.

(3) The Archeological, and this has naturally many branches, each of which has the character of a learned inquiry calling for special knowledge, and, in many instances, only of limited interest outside the field of scholarship. The archaeology of the legend would include, of course, its sources, which remain debatable, and certain problems of authorship in connection with the early romances, as, for example, whether Master Blihis did write the first Percival in the latter half of the 13th century. The Grail in the musical epics of Wagner has been the subject of special devotion in the writings of Miss Jessie L. Watson. Outside these admitted branches of research there is a fourth point of view which has emerged more recently, and for want of a better term may, perhaps, be called Spiritual. It cares little for the archaeology of the subject, little for the romantic aspects and as little perhaps, explicitly, for the

poetic side. It would know nothing of Hawker's "Quest," and would regard the Grail simply as one of the sacramental legends of the soul; yet it is not confined, nor is it indeed found, to any important extent, among those who hold extreme Eucharistic views. In other words, it is not specially a high Anglican or a Latin interest; it is found rather among those who regard religious doctrine, institution and ritual, as things typical or analogical, and the Grail as an early recognition of the fact that such things are really symbols and not for literal acceptance. This view cares, perhaps, only in an ordinary degree for the evidences of history, nor can history be said to endorse it. It is a consideration of certain devout minds. Connected with this, although really independent, there is a still more recent disposition to regard the whole legend as hinting at the perpetuation of a secret teaching within the Christian church which is not exactly what is understood commonly by Christianity. There is much to be said for this view, though in the form that we at present possess it, it may be admitted that it still awaits demonstration. There is perhaps a certain sense in which all these views can be accepted, and in which all are capable in the last resource of being harmonized together. No one can read the romances without seeing that the legend has its spiritual side, but it has also, and not less evidently, that side which connects it with folklore. In the hands of the compiler of the "Morte d'Arthur" it is treated openly as an allegory, and the knighthood of King Arthur's Court passes explicitly during the quest into a region of similitude, where every adventure and episode has a supernatural signification which is explained sometimes in rather a tiresome manner. On the other hand, in the romance of Sir Percival, there are assuredly traces of a doctrine or system which is not quite in affinity with the Christianity of its period, and there is also a suggestion of veiled hostility to the church of that period.

The Legend of the Holy Grail and its Connection with Templars and Freemasons

Part IV

Sources of the Legend

The sources of the romance-legend are of two kinds, existing and traditional, the second class being represented only by the tradition of a Latin MS., which is referred to by most narrators of the legend, with the exception of Sir Thomas Malory, though it is possible that they have borrowed the reference from one another. On the authority, by no means unquestionable, of a certain chronicle of Helinandus, this book was entitled "Liber Gradalis" and was the work of a British hermit, whose name does not transpire. Moreover, it had not been seen by the historian who mentions it. At the present day it is regarded as mythical by scholars, but, after making every allowance, there does not, perhaps, seem full ground for doubting the fact of its existence. It is pointed out that there are no romance works in the Latin language, but this is not a valid objection, because it does not follow that the Latin original was in the form which we naturally attribute to the word romance. This word originally involved a work written in the romance language, and everything points, as regards the Latin manuscript, to the fact that it was rather in the nature of an apocryphal gospel book, as indeed its imputed authorship would imply, and as such it is not impossible that it may still exist among the uninvestigated treasures of old monastic libraries in the remote corners of Brittany.

The extant sources may be summarized as follows:—

(1) The mediaeval poem of the Grail, begun by Chrestien

de Troyes who died between 1181 and 1190, and of whose work there are several continuations which may have been written at any time between the close of the twelfth and the middle of the thirteenth century.

(2) The romance poem of Joseph of Arimathea, very nearly perfect, a single leaf only being wanting in one of the most complete copies. The author was Robert de Borron, who wrote it towards the end of the twelfth century, and died in 1212.

(3) The prose version of this poem, which supplies the defect therein; although in respect of the language it corresponds, like the poem, to the original meaning of the term romance, it is not of the kind which we understand by the word—that is to say—both versions purport to be true histories and are in fact a species of apocryphal narrative, somewhat approaching the canonical Acts of the Apostles, giving the genealogy of Joseph and all his descendants with a pseudo history of his life, travels and imprisonments before and after the Ascension of Christ.

(4) A sequel to the poem of Borron by a later hand, known as the Didot Percival, of which there is only a single manuscript in existence.

(5) The quest of the San Grail, corresponding in all respects to what the ordinary literate reader would understand by the romance of chivalry. It is the most famous of the whole cycle.

(6) The romance of Sir Percival le Gallois, which of recent years has come into the hands of many thousands of English readers in the translation of Dr. Sebastian Evans. This is an elaborate, highly pictorial narrative of the best romantic kind, and it contains the presumptive evidence out of which the present hypothesis has arisen.

(7) Sir Thomas Malory's "Birth, Life and Acts of King Arthur," more commonly known under the name of "Morte d'Arthur." It was originally printed by Caxton and the modern editions are numerous. The Quest of the Grail (see *ante*, No. 5) occupies several books of this great compilation, to the production of which a singular genius was brought by the compiler, and it is and will remain one of the great epoch making books of English literature. Sir Edward Strachey, one of its modern editors, has well pointed out that the narrative is almost epical in its form, and has so digested the confused materials on which Malory wrought, that something of sustained purpose appears throughout, and it has, so to speak, a beginning, middle and end.

(8) A distinct cycle of the Grail Legend is filled by the German romances, as already noted. Their place is a little difficult to settle on satisfactory grounds. Some French scholars have endeavored to show that the source of the Arthurian legends is to be sought in Germany, but it is a hypothesis advanced b those who seek to minimize their merit in favor of the superior claims of the Charlemagne cycle, and this does not bear consideration. The German cycle may be classified as follows:-

A. The Romance of Titurel.

B. That of Parsifal.

C. That of Lohengrin.

They are all interconnected, and the order given above is in a sense almost chronological. Titurel was the first knight called to the guarding of the Grail, and is supposed to have built a temple in which it was placed during the period that it abode on Earth. Parsifal is of course the German version of Percival, and Lohengrin is the latest and closing legend, corresponding to that of Galahad in the "Morte d'Arthur," in which, however, the chronological succession is entirely lost.

(9) For the sake of completeness two other romances may be mentioned: that of Peredur, the son of Earl Evrawe, a Welsh legend of the thirteenth century or earlier, and the English metrical romance of Sir Percyvelle; but they do not call for consideration in the present connection.

It should be added that the above list is not chronologically arranged.

The Legend of the Holy Grail and its Connection with Templars and Freemasons

Part V

The Secret of the Grail

Whatever the elements which entered into the composition of the Grail conception, all the chief versions of the legend unite in connecting it with the mystery and power of certain secret words. These words, in the earlier romances, are entrusted by Christ Himself to the custody of Joseph of Arimathea. Those who can acquire and retain them, can exercise at will a strange power and mastery over all about them and will possess great credit in the sight of God. They never need fear being deprived of their rights, sufferings from evil judgment, or conquest in battle, so long as their cause is just. It is impossible, however, to communicate these words in writing; they are too precious and holy, and, moreover, they are the secret of the Grail itself, in which a strange power of speech also resides. Joseph himself was only permitted to reveal them to a single person, a mysterious rich fisherman who figures continually in the stories, sometimes following the craft which his name suggests, sometimes as the lord of a stately castle, in several instances as a king. He, in his turn, and by virtue of some mysterious power or license vested in him, does appear to have committed them to writing, together with other secrets, but they are to be concealed forever from the world.

In the prologue or preamble of the Grand San Grail legend, the hermit who receives the revelations and the custody of the mysterious book of the legend, testifies that the greatest secret of the world has been confided to him, and that the communication took place amidst inexpressible experiences in that third heaven to which St. Paul was translated. The description of his ecstasy is written in fervent language. On the other hand, in the Didot Percival, the putative sequel to the poems of Robert de Borron, the secret words appear as those which Christ spoke to Joseph on the Cross. After they have been imparted to one of the heroes of the story, he is translated by angels. It is needless to add that the maker of this chronicle is forbidden to transcribe them.

In another class of the romances the unutterable words reappear in a simplified or substituted form, and we have in this manner the legends of a suppressed word, of the sorrow and the misery which is wrought by that suppression, and of the joy and the deliverance which follow the utterance of the word, whereby great enchantments are determined, great wrongs redressed, and the wounds and sufferings endured through many years are healed and annulled. This mystery of the word which is withheld, or in reservation, would offer some curious points to criticism if the subject could be pursued here. It takes the form of a simple question which should have been asked and was not, and as such it is, so to speak, the reverse side or antithesis of the old classical legend of the sphinx. The sphinx asked questions and devoured those who did not reply, or whose answers blundered. Percival in the romances kept silence, when he should have urged his inquiries, sometimes through carelessness, sometimes through false modesty, sometimes because he had been cautioned against idle questioning, but in all cases indifferently, by the working of some apparently blind destiny, the omission carries with it the long series of its disastrous consequences.

The higher sense of the mysterious word or words is of course removed to heaven when the Grail is itself removed, the departure of which is described in many ways, of which the following from the "Morte d'Arthur" may serve as an example. *"And when he had said these words Galahad went to Percival and kissed him and commended him to God, and so he went to Sir Bors, and kissed him, and commended him to God, and said, Fair lord, salute me to my lord Sir Lancelot, my father, and as soon as you see him, bid him remember of this unstable world. And therewith he kneeled down before the table, and made his prayers, and then suddenly his soul departed to Jesu Christ and a great multitude of angels bore his soul up to heaven, that the two fellows might well behold it. Also the two fellows saw come from heaven an hand, but they saw not the body. And then it came right to the vessel, and took it and the spear, and so bare it up to heaven. Since then was there never man so hardy to say that he had seen the Sangraal."* But the lesser word, the word which can be withheld or spoken, has performed in the meantime a certain office of amelioration, so that it is not by a mere vain observance that it has been in a sense substituted by the later romances for that which could neither be spelt nor written.

Of such is the Grail Legend, and those who are acquainted with it in the most choice of its early forms will agree not only that many portions of it are singularly winning, but that it is indeed

"*a part Of the hunger and thirst of the heart.*"

It is also a very melancholy legend; it is the passing of a great procession and a great sacrament which is destined never to return; it is a portion of the loss of humanity; and it is no matter for surprise that in these late days which are so full of this thirst and this hunger, several persons have attempted to read into it a more profound significance than could have been consciously intended by its makers.

The Legend of the Holy Grail and its Connection with Templars and Freemasons

Part VI
The Templar Connection

The slight investigation here attempted has proceeded so far solely on the basis of the documents, though it must be admitted that, as regards the last section there has not been any special attention paid to the subject by English scholars. The Templar connections of the Grail Legend lie also on the face of the documents, but these are recognized by scholarship. Some are trivial in themselves, but are noticeable by their continual recurrence throughout the romances, as, for example, the characteristic Templar symbolism of the white alb and the scarlet cross, varied by the scarlet cross on the white banner, or on the white sails of fairy ships, and so forth. Other connections are rooted more deeply and of great significance. There are indications of a confraternity, partly military and partly religious, connecting by the legend of a lineage with a kind of secret history of Christendom, written under the guise of knight errantry. This feature is more especially noticeable in the German versions. The later adaptations of the Lohengrin Legend are literally and verbally Templar, but the German Parsifal, written by Wolfram von Eschenbach, prior to 1215, is the romance of a brotherhood of the Holy Grail, strong, mighty and powerful, while that of Titurel is the legend of the building of a Temple. And this leads to a still more important point, also fully acknowledged by scholars, namely, that current through all the stories we have the hint of the existence of what has been termed a Grail Church, that is to say, of a secret doctrine which, by the hypothesis, is higher than the open doctrine which at the time was taught in Christendom. The inmost heart of this doctrine is no doubt typically represented by the Grail itself, and in accordance with this view, it will be sufficient to point out the amazing statement that the Eucharist was first entrusted to Joseph of Arimathea, that he was the first priest who ever celebrated the Mass and was the first bishop of the Church, consecrated by Christ himself and the angels. The book of the Grail also claims Christ as its author and thus stands in a position of inexpressible superiority to the gospels. Behind this blasphemous ascription, which in itself could not have been literally intended, there could be only the implied existence of some concealed instruction of religion, which claimed for itself a more sacred sanction than that of orthodox Christianity. Equally designed to enforce this claim, and signifying equally something which did not appear on the surface, is the pretense that among the treasures of the Grail Church were the crown and sword of David and the wood of the Tree of Life. The precise intention of these allegories may perhaps never be unraveled, but their general design is apparent, and this corresponds broadly to the chief accusations brought against the Knights Templar at the time of their suppression. The two centuries of their existence are also the two centuries during which the Grail legends were originated and for the most part developed. Most of the accusations raised against the brethren were not so much unfounded as baser constructed, and after every allowance has been made, there is reasonable ground for inferring that they acquired strange knowledge in the East, on the basis of which they raised claims to a priestly and religious preeminence, and these claims found in the romances of the west, which seem to have been inspired by them and to have grown up to some extent under their auspices, an indirect and veiled expression.

The specific considerations which tend towards the substantiation of this view are of course highly technical, and they involve issues which have been long and hotly debated. There is, firstly, so much light as can be obtained from the name of the order and from the improbability of the pretense that it was so called because its first house was situated near the site of King Solomon's Temple. It is advanced that the Knights were brethren of the Temple in a less accidental sense, and were secretly pledged to the erection, symbolically speaking, of another house of God which was neither precisely of Israel nor of Christendom. In this connection there is a legend of Solomon within the Grail legend which calls for the elucidation of scholarship; but there is, above all, the fact that the Grail heroes were Temple-builders. Secondly, there is the use among the Templars of secret words which did not carry their significance on their surface, and were therefore, in a sense, substituted words, by which the true and more secret words were suppressed and concealed from the lower ranks of the brethren. In the third place, amongst alleged Templar remains, there are examples of fonts or vases which have been regarded as Grail vessels, and in this connection it may be noted, because of the alleged sympathies between the Templars and some of the survivals of the Gnostic sects, that, according to Epiphanius, the Marcosian heretics made use of similar vases in their celebration of the Eucharist. They were filled with white wine, which was supposed to undergo transformations of color and other magical changes which recall the marvelous permutations of the Grail cup in the old books of chivalry.

But the most important consideration of the whole is one which so far has passed entirely unnoticed, and this is, that about the period when the Grail romances may be supposed to have originated, the Latin Church denied the Chalice to the laity, and Communion was limited to one kind. Is it too much to suppose, that when the most sacred rite and highest sacrament of the Christian religion was thus tampered with, and, in appearance, violated, there must have arisen a very strong feeling of hostility? Is it too much to suppose, when about the same period we find a cycle of legend springing into existence, the central point of which was the very Cup Of Mystery which was thus withheld from the faithful, that between the two there is some connection corresponding to cause and effect? And at the back of this hostility, and at the back of these legends, is there any class of society at the period more possible, and even probable, than those Knights Templar who were themselves a priestly order, to whom as such the Communion in both kinds was doubtless continued, and to whom the Eucharistic rite seems in some form always to have been a special object of veneration?

As, on the one hand, it is by no means pretended that this account does common justice to an exceedingly complex subject, so on the other, it cannot be affirmed that the fullest analogies would lead up to a demonstration in the existing state of knowledge. But after every allowance has been made for the greed and duplicity of the French King, who coveted the Templar possessions, and for the criminal weakness of the servile Pontiff who acted as his tool, there is much to be said for the view, that the Church and perhaps the State were guided by no mistaken instinct when they regarded the Templar pretensions as inimical to their own safety, and so also, amidst much exaggeration and much invention, their enemies of latter days, the Romish historians, who have connected the order with the Gnostics, the Manicheans, the Albigenses and kindred heresies which overran several parts of Europe when the Templars were at the height of their power, may not have been so profoundly mistaken as has been sometimes supposed.

The Legend of the Holy Grail and its Connection with Templars and Freemasons

Part VII
The Connection With Masonry

The theory that Masonry of the speculative kind was developed somehow from the Building Guilds, explains very little of itself, and to speak of its comparative simplicity, which is that which has recommended it chiefly, is not really to press one of its advantages. Those who adopt it will have in the end to admit, as already indicated, that the operative craft was assumed by persons who were not operative Masons, and this is all that is asked for by the Templar or any other hypothesis. At present, and after the persistent investigations of many generations less or more equipped for the purpose, it must he confessed that speculative Freemasonry is still in the position of Melchizedek, without father or mother; but so far as presumptive evidence is concerned, the Templar explanation is not in reality more difficult than any Of its competitors, if it can be shown that the knightly order survived the destruction which was attempted by the Pope and the King. And as to this no two opinions are really possible, and those who maintain the negative are doing but little better than playing with the words. For, in the first place, the Order in Portugal was never suppressed at all, but was transformed into the Order of Christ. In the second place there was no suppression in Germany in the sense that we attach to the term, and there the Knights Templar became the Teutonic Knights, though there is a break in the succession. In the third place, there are several other countries where the proscription was partial and halfhearted only, and, lastly, in Scotland there is valid ground for believing that the quarrels of the Scottish king with his English neighbor were at that period far too strenuous to admit of his interfering with an Order of Knighthood from which he had better reason to look for material assistance. The suppression, no doubt, in France, and in some other countries, took the form of practical destruction, but even there the apologists of the Latin Church, who also figure among those who maintain the complete overthrow of the Fraternity, are the first to deny that anything like the majority of the Knights Templar suffered more than the ordinary canonical punishments of the period. Now it is precisely in Scotland that the consistent tradition of modern Templarism points to the continuation of the old Order, and later on to its identification with the Operative Masonry of that country. Here, again, the evidences are practically impossible to summarize, as they would involve a minute examination not only of many historical documents, real or alleged, but also of the Templar Rituals of Masonry, and of the literature which has grown out of the claim. The following statements have been advanced on historical ground. In 1309, the Grand Preceptor of Scotland was Walter de Clifton, who subsequently became Grand Master, and five years later the Templars joined the standard of the Bruce, and being instrumental in placing him on the throne, their former grants were confirmed by him. The Templars are mentioned in two charters, one of which is dated 1340, and the other about a century later. They are now in possession of the Chapter General of Scotland. In the reign of James IV, there was a union of the Templars and Hospitallers, the evidence for which is a charter dated October 19th, 1488, confirming grants of lands to the Knights of the Temple and St. john. After the Act of 1560 prohibiting allegiance to Rome, Sir William Sandilands, Preceptor of Torphichen, and successor to Sir William Lindsay as Master of the Temple, gave territories of both Orders to the State, which were then made over to him, with the lordship of Torphichen, in return for a certain payment. The Knights thereupon drew off in a body with the Grand Prior, David Seton. We must turn, however, from special points to an indication of the wider lines of the argument, which, to put it as shortly as possible, takes in the first place the Masonic legend of Hiram, which is that of the Third Degree, and refers it, with the majority of Masonic historians, to its prototype in the Compagnonage or Building Guilds of France; it connects the Compagnonage itself through Templarism with the religious sects of the South of Europe, who drew like the Templars from the East; it seeks to show that modern Masonry deriving, as it is allowed, from the one is also referable to the other. We are concerned, however, with an analogy which is more important for our purpose, and having shown that, according to the best scholarship of the present period, the Grail legends exhibit Templar marks, and possess Templar connections, it remains to indicate that the Masonic legend is but another version of what has been termed here the Secret of the Grail.

The great and chief legend of Masonry, which is that of the Third Degree, the head and crown of the symbolic edifice, gives account of the circumstances under which a great and sacred knowledge summarized in a word of mysterious power was lost through a deed of treason, since which time, as in the Grail Legend, a substituted word only is conferred upon the candidate, to be kept in his heart until the restoration of the true word. The latter, also like the Grail Legend, is one of Divine power and is actually the building word of the first Master Mason, who died rather than communicate it, much after the same manner as we find it stated in the romance legends. In a supplementary degree, called the Royal Arch, the Lost Word is ostensibly recovered, but as a fact the word imparted is only another substitute. There are also other grades belonging to various classes and sources, all passing under the name of High Grades, being superadded to the original Craft degrees, and in many of these the true word is supposed to be found and joy restored to the seekers, even as in the Grail Legends the punishments and sufferings were removed; but they are all of the same character, that is to say, they are merely makeshifts and evasions. The true initiates of masonry, of whom there are comparatively speaking very few, know well the reason, which is that given by the hermit in the preamble of the Grand San Grail, namely, that the last secrets are incommunicable; but they know also that they exist. In any case this loss and this alleged restoration are the whole concern of Masonic symbolism; they are that to which the profane person cannot penetrate, at least by the hypothesis. There is, therefore, from the Masonic standpoint, a lost knowledge which Masonry assuredly memorizes, and which the Worshipful Master, in the charge to the candidate who has been raised to the Third Degree, confesses to be lost, even as the Holy Grail was removed from earth, and for the same reason, that is to say, on account of the unworthiness of the world. The building word of the Master Architect was removed when he was slain, and though the Temple was finished by a species of substitution, it was not after the original plan. Thus the Masonic legend, like that of the Grail histories, has throughout a note of sadness and of want. The echoes of the old legend of Eden, so often referred to by the makers of the romances, the memory of that loss which is the world's loss, reverberate through the mysteries of the Building Craft, uplifted into the sphere of symbols, dimly and unaccountably.

Such are the outlines of the analogy which it has been sought to establish. It is not pretended that it approaches demonstration, but merely that it offers an interesting light on obscure fields of research, and that something has been accomplished towards showing that the mystery of secret teaching hinted at almost everywhere in the Grail legends, the mystery which has for centuries shrouded the inner teaching imparted by the Templar initiation, and the mystery which involves the origin of the great legend of Masonry are not in reality three mysteries, but rather a single mystery exhibited through various vehicles. The further elucidation of the problem must be left to specialists of the several branches of research, which, if even for a moment only, it has so unexpectedly brought together.

Alchemy of the Rosicrucians

by Jerome A. Anderson

It has become the accepted thing to explain the assertion of the Rosicrucian philosophers that the baser metals may be transmuted into gold by claiming that this refers to the changing of the lower animal nature into the spiritual gold of love and compassion. But there are always seven keys to the truth concealed beneath any allegory, and the half-veiled teaching of the mystery of transmutation is no exception. The changing of the selfish passions into unselfishness by means of the awakened spiritual will is a *correct* reading of the meaning of these philosophers, but it is not the only one.

There is a deeper significance to the teaching. These wise old Fire-philosophers concealed a cosmic philosophy beneath an allegory so simple in its cunning that it only aroused the cupidity of the selfish, and the contempt of those wise in their own conceit. This philosophy may be stated thus:

There is but one consciousness in the universe; it is infinite, and all the differing states of consciousness in nature are its finite manifestations. Similarly, all forms of matter, and all modes of force, are but finite manifestations of an Infinite Source of energy and matter. That which is infinite *can* only manifest itself finitely through infinite diversity, and so consciousness, matter and force are but the infinitely diversified aspects of infinite Unity.

From the material aspect of Nature, this unity in source and essence of all its myriads of forms is easily proven, and the

Rosicrucian philosophers, having done so for themselves, sought to teach the great truth under the allegory of the transmutation of metals. One has but to accept their hint to perceive that transmutation is plainly taught in the alchemy of Nature and its processes demonstrated at every moment of life.

The examination may be begun at any portion of the arc of the manifesting cycle. Selecting the mineral kingdom, the frost and rain are seen rending the rock into fragments; the attrition of these under the action of water, producing sands and clays; a seed lodges thereon and a mighty monarch of the forest up rears its form directly out of and from the mineral kingdom. It has arisen out of that which as rock, clay, water or air gave no hint that it contained such a divine possibility. Some unseen force has transformed the apparently lifeless rock into the living tree. No new thing has been added; only that which eternally *Is* has been used. Truly, some mighty chemist has been busying himself in the workshop of Nature, and, while the finished product is accepted and admired, recognition is refused of either the alchemist or his processes. Yet there has been a divinely wonderful thing accomplished — the transformation of the inorganic into the organic; a weaving of the fiber of the rock into the cells of the tree. No trace of the old rock appears in the new product, yet the basic substance in both must have been the same, else there can only be supposed an annihilation of the one and a new creation of the other.

Scientists perceive something of this mysterious transmutation, and seek vainly for the basic substance from which Nature must have sprung. The search will be in vain so long as it gropes in matter only. The indestructibility of matter and the conservation of energy, broad and generalizing truths as they are, will not bridge a chasm which only consciousness can cross. Or rather, the inseparableness of consciousness, force and matter, as eternal aspects of one basic unity, must be recognized and accepted as a starting point in the search after truth. Then it will be perceived that eternal transmutation is the process of Nature, and the real meaning of the sayings of the Fire-philosophers will dawn upon the mind.

For creation is transmutation. Of a surety, there has been, and is, a new creation with every gas that condenses into a rock, with every flower that blooms from the heart of the unyielding granite, with each form of man or animal built by means of these earlier transmutations. There never has been, there never can be, other creation than this transmutation of the lower "same" into the higher "other" of Plato. And he who is wise enough and strong enough to control, direct, and *reverse* Nature's processes may easily disintegrate the base metal back to a common, primal source, and then re-integrate it as gold, with no greater effort than that which he now puts forth in his effort to change human hate into godlike love.

That which is thus seen to be true in relation to the material aspect is equally true of the conscious aspect of the Absolute. For this is only the same infinite Unity, making itself known as another finite concept. The same consciousness is at the base of that in the rock, and that of the very highest archangel: the consciousness apparently benumbed in the one may be transmuted into that of the other. It *is* being so transmuted; it is in the eternal plan, and it is the work of the eternal eons, to slowly bring about the wondrous change.

Looking backward in Nature, man may perceive the states of consciousness out of which he has crept; looking forward, he may perceive those which await him. The very highest state of consciousness of which he can conceive he may reach through this divine process. The wisdom to image forth, and the power to transform, are his. The glorious certainty that consciousness is ONE, and that the very highest creative consciousness whose efforts he perceives in nature about him may be his, lies revealed in the transformation of the lowly daisy out of something which it was and yet was not. Worlds may wing their way through space in obedience to his human will, once he has transmuted that will into and united it with that of the Supreme.

The changing of selfishness into unselfishness in one's daily life is but a preparatory transmutation, even as the grinding of the rock preceded the formation of the soil which made the tree possible. Making the flowers of human kindness spring along his pathway is but the prophecy of the time when they may actually do so, as is told in the myths of the gods of old. And man *is* a god, for his being roots in that which he may transmute into godhood; he is a finite god because he has but begun the transmutation. As Those beyond him have, with infinite love and patience, transmuted the fiery star-dust into a world and a mantle of flesh for him, so must he, with equally infinite love and patience, transmute the base metal of his lower nature into the gold of spiritual life.

Initiation, the Ancient Mysteries and the Dionysiac Artificers

by Albert G. Mackey

I now propose, for the purpose of illustrating these views, and of familiarizing the reader with the coincidences between Freemasonry and the ancient Mysteries, so that he may be better enabled to appreciate the mutual influences of each on the other as they are hereafter to be developed, to present a more detailed relation of one or more of these ancient systems of initiation.

As the first illustration, let us select the Mysteries of Osiris, as they were practiced in Egypt, the birthplace of all that is wonderful in the arts or sciences, or mysterious in the religion, of the ancient world.

It was on the Lake of Sais that the solemn ceremonies of the Osirian initiation were performed. "On this lake," says Herodotus, "it is that the Egyptians represent by night his sufferings whose name I refrain from mentioning; and this representation they call their Mysteries."

Osiris, the husband of Isis, was an ancient king of the Egyptians. Having been slain by Typhon, his body was cut into pieces by his murderer, and the mangled remains cast upon the waters of the Nile, to be dispersed to the four winds of heaven. His wife, Isis, mourning for the death and the mutilation of her husband, for many days searched diligently with her companions for the portions of the body, and having at length found them, united them together, and bestowed upon them decent interment,—while Osiris, thus restored, became the chief deity of his subjects, and his worship was united with that of Isis, as the fecundating and fertilizing powers of nature. The candidate in these initiations was made to pass through a mimic repetition of the conflict and destruction of Osiris, and his eventual recovery; and the explanations made to him, after he had received the full share of light to which the painful and solemn ceremonies through which he had passed had entitled him, constituted the secret doctrine of which I have already spoken, as the object of all the Mysteries. Osiris,—a real and personal god to the people,—to be worshipped with fear and with trembling, and to be propitiated with sacrifices and burnt offerings, became to the initiate but a symbol of the "Great first cause, least understood," while his death, and the wailing of Isis, with the recovery of the body, his translation to the rank of a celestial being, and the consequent rejoicing of his spouse, were but a tropical mode of teaching that after death comes life eternal, and that though the body be destroyed, the soul shall still live.

"Can we doubt," says the Baron Sainte Croix, "that such ceremonies as those practiced in the Mysteries of Osiris had been originally instituted to impress more profoundly on the mind the dogma of future rewards and punishments?"

"The sufferings and death of Osiris," says Mr. Wilkinson, "were the great Mystery of the Egyptian religion; and some traces of it are perceptible among other people of antiquity. His being the divine goodness and the abstract idea of 'good,' his manifestation upon earth (like an Indian god), his death and resurrection, and his office as judge of the dead in a future state, look like the early revelation of a future manifestation of the deity converted into a mythological fable."

A similar legend and similar ceremonies, varied only as to time, and place, and unimportant details, were to be found in all the initiations of the ancient Mysteries. The dogma was the same,—future life,—and the method of inculcating it was the same. The coincidences between the design of these rites and that of Freemasonry, which must already begin to appear, will enable us to give its full value to the expression of Hutchinson, when he says that "the Master Mason represents a man under the Christian doctrine saved from the grave of iniquity and raised to the faith of salvation."

In Phoenicia similar Mysteries were celebrated in honor of Adonis, the favorite lover of Venus, who, having, while hunting, been slain by a wild boar on Mount Lebanon, was restored to life by Proserpine. The mythological story is familiar to every classical scholar. In the popular theology, Adonis was the son of Cinyras, king of Cyrus, whose untimely death was wept by Venus and her attendant nymphs: in the physical theology of the philosophers, he was a symbol of the sun, alternately present to and absent from the earth; but in the initiation into the Mysteries of his worship, his resurrection and return from Hades were adopted as a type of the immortality of the soul. The ceremonies of initiation in the Adonia began with lamentation for his loss,—or, as the prophet Ezekiel expresses it, "Behold, there sat women weeping for Thammuz,"—for such was the name under which his worship was introduced among the Jews; and they ended with the most extravagant demonstrations of joy at the representation of his return to life, while the hierophant exclaimed, in a congratulatory strain,— "Trust, ye initiates; the god is safe, And from our grief salvation shall arise."

Before proceeding to an examination of those Mysteries which are the most closely connected with the masonic institution, it will be as well to take a brief view of their general organization.

The secret worship, or Mysteries, of the ancients were always divided into the lesser and the greater; the former being intended only to awaken curiosity, to test the capacity and disposition of the candidate, and by symbolical purifications to prepare him for his introduction into the greater Mysteries.

The candidate was at first called an aspirant, or seeker of the truth, and the initial ceremony which he underwent was a lustration or purification by water. In this condition he may be compared to the Entered Apprentice of the masonic rites, and it is here worth adverting to the fact (which will be hereafter more fully developed) that all the ceremonies in the first degree of masonry are symbolic of an internal purification.

In the lesser Mysteries the candidate took an oath of secrecy, which was administered to him by the mystagogue, and then received a preparatory instruction, which enabled him afterwards to understand the developments of the higher and subsequent division. He was now called a *Mystes*, or initiate, and may be compared to the Fellow Craft of Freemasonry.

In the greater Mysteries the whole knowledge of the divine truths, which was the object of initiation, was communicated. Here we find, among the various ceremonies which assimilated these rites to Freemasonry, the *aphanism*, which was the disappearance or death; the *pastos*, the couch, coffin, or grave; the *euresis*, or the discovery of the body; and the *autopsy*, or full sight of everything, that is, the complete communication of the secrets. The candidate was here called an *epopt*, or eye-witness, because nothing was now hidden from him; and hence he may be compared to the Master Mason, of whom Hutchinson says that "he has discovered the knowledge of God and his salvation, and been redeemed from the death of sin and the sepulchre of pollution and unrighteousness."

After this general view of the religious Mysteries of the ancient world, let us now proceed to a closer examination of those which are more intimately connected with the history of Freemasonry, and whose influence is, to this day, most evidently felt in its organization.

Of all the pagan Mysteries instituted by the ancients none were more extensively diffused than those of the Grecian god Dionysus. They were established in Greece, Rome, Syria, and all Asia Minor. Among the Greeks, and still more among the Romans, the rites celebrated on the Dionysiac festival were, it must be confessed, of a dissolute and licentious character. But in Asia they assumed a different form. There, as elsewhere, the legend (for it has already been said that each Mystery had its legend) recounted, and the ceremonies represented, the murder of Dionysus by the Titans. The secret doctrine, too, among the Asiatics, was not different from that among the western nations, but there was something peculiar in the organization of the system. The Mysteries of Dionysus in Syria, more especially, were not simply of a theological character. There the disciples joined to the indulgence in their speculative and secret opinions as to the unity of God and the immortality of the soul, which were common to all the Mysteries, the practice of an operative and architectural art, and occupied themselves as well in the construction of temples and public buildings as in the pursuit of divine truth.

I can account for the greater purity of these Syrian rites only by adopting the ingenious theory of Thirwall, that all the Mysteries "were the remains of a worship which preceded the rise of the Hellenic mythology, and its attendant rites, grounded on a view of nature less fanciful, more earnest, and better fitted to awaken both philosophical thought and religious feeling," and by supposing that the Asiatics, not being, from their geographical position, so early imbued with the errors of Hellenism, had been better able to preserve the purity and philosophy of the old Pelasgic faith, which, itself, was undoubtedly a direct emanation from the patriarchal religion, or, as it has been called, the Pure Freemasonry of the antediluvian world.

Be this, however, as it may, we know that "the Dionysiacs of Asia Minor were undoubtedly an association of architects and engineers, who had the exclusive privilege of building temples, stadia, and theatres, under the mysterious tutelage of Bacchus, and were distinguished from the uninitiated or profane inhabitants by the science which they possessed, and by many private signs and tokens by which they recognized each other."

This speculative and operative society—speculative in the esoteric, theologic lessons which were taught in its initiations, and operative in the labors of its members as architects—was distinguished by many peculiarities that closely assimilate it to the institution of Freemasonry. In the practice of charity, the more opulent were bound to relieve the wants and contribute to the support of the poorer brethren. They were divided, for the conveniences of labor and the advantages of government, into smaller bodies, which, like our lodges, were directed by superintending officers. They employed, in their ceremonial observances, many of the implements of operative Masonry, and used, like the Masons, a universal language; and conventional modes of recognition, by which *one brother might know another in the dark as well as the light*, and which served to unite the whole body, wheresoever they might be dispersed, in one common brotherhood.

I have said that in the mysteries of Dionysus the legend recounted the death of that hero-god, and the subsequent discovery of his body. Some further details of the nature of the Dionysiac ritual are, therefore, necessary for a thorough appreciation of the points to which I propose directly to invite attention.

In these mystic rites, the aspirant was made to represent, symbolically and in a dramatic form, the events connected with the slaying of the god from whom the Mysteries derived their name. After a variety of preparatory ceremonies, intended to call forth all his courage and fortitude, the aphanism or mystical death of Dionysus was figured out in the ceremonies, and the shrieks and lamentations of the initiates, with the confinement or burial of the candidate on the pastos, couch, or coffin, constituted the first part of the ceremony of initiation. Then began the search of Rhea for the remains of Dionysus, which was continued amid scenes of the greatest confusion and tumult, until, at last, the search having been successful, the mourning was turned into joy, light succeeded to darkness, and the candidate was invested with the knowledge of the secret doctrine of the Mysteries—the belief in the existence of one God, and a future state of rewards and punishments.

Such were the mysteries that were practised by the architect,—the Freemasons, so to speak—of Asia Minor. At Tyre, the richest and most important city of that region, a city memorable for the splendor and magnificence of the buildings with which it was decorated, there were colonies or lodges of these mystic architects; and this fact I request that you will bear in mind, as it forms an important link in the chain that connects the Dionysiacs with the Freemasons.

But to make every link in this chain of connection complete, it is necessary that the mystic artists of Tyre should be proved to be at least contemporaneous with the building of King Solomon's temple; and the evidence of that fact I shall now attempt to produce.

Lawrie, whose elaborate researches into this subject leave us nothing further to discover, places the arrival of the Dionysiacs in Asia Minor at the time of the Ionic migration, when "the inhabitants of Attica, complaining of the narrowness of their territory and the unfruitfulness of its soil, went in quest of more extensive and fertile settlements. Being joined by a number of the inhabitants of surrounding provinces, they sailed to Asia Minor, drove out the original inhabitants, and seized upon the most eligible situations, and united them under the name of Ionia, because the greatest number of the refugees were natives of that Grecian province." With their knowledge of the arts of sculpture and architecture, in which the Greeks had already made some progress, the emigrants brought over to their new settlements their religious customs also, and introduced into Asia the mysteries of Athena and Dionysus long before they had been corrupted by the licentiousness of the mother country.

Now, Playfair places the Ionic migration in the year 1044 B.C., Gillies in 1055, and the Abbé Barthelemy in 1076. But the latest of these periods will extend as far back as forty-four years before the commencement of the temple of Solomon at Jerusalem, and will give ample time for the establishment of the Dionysiac fraternity at the city of Tyre, and the initiation of "Hiram the Builder" into its mysteries.

Let us now pursue the chain of historical events which finally united this purest branch of the Spurious Freemasonry of the pagan nations with the Primitive Freemasonry of the Jews at Jerusalem.

When Solomon, king of Israel, was about to build, in accordance with the purposes of his father, David, "a house unto the name of Jehovah, his God," he made his intention known to Hiram, king of Tyre, his friend and ally; and because he was well aware of the architectural skill of the Tyrian Dionysiacs, he besought that monarch's assistance to enable him to carry his pious design into execution. Scripture informs us that Hiram complied with the request of Solomon, and sent him the necessary workmen to assist him in the glorious undertaking. Among others, he sent an architect, who is briefly described, in the First Book of Kings, as "a widow's son, of the tribe of Naphtali, and his father a man of Tyre, a worker in brass, a man filled with wisdom and understanding and cunning to work all works in brass;" and more fully, in the Second Book of Chronicles, as "a cunning man, endued with understanding of Hiram my father's, the son of a woman of the daughters of Dan, and his father, a man of Tyre, skillful to work in gold, and in silver, in brass, in iron, in stone, and in timber, in purple, in blue, and in fine linen and in crimson, also to grave any manner of graving, and to find out any device which shall be put to him."

To this man—this widow's son (as Scripture history, as well as masonic tradition informs us)—was entrusted by King Solomon an important position among the workmen at the sacred edifice, which was constructed on Mount Moriah. His knowledge and experience as an artificer, and his eminent skill in every kind of "curious and cunning workmanship," readily placed him at the head of both the Jewish and Tyrian craftsmen, as the chief builder and principal conductor of the works; and it is to him, by means of the large authority which this position gave him, that we attribute the union of two people, so antagonistical in race, so dissimilar in manners, and so opposed in religion, as the Jews and Tyrians, in one common brotherhood, which resulted in the organization of the institution of Freemasonry. This Hiram, as a Tyrian and an artificer, must have been connected with the Dionysiac fraternity; nor could he have been a very humble or inconspicuous member, if we may judge of his rank in the society, from the amount of talent which he is said to have possessed, and from the elevated position that he held in the affections, and at the court, of the king of Tyre. He must, therefore, have been well acquainted with all the ceremonial usages of the Dionysiac artificers, and must have enjoyed a long experience of the advantages of the government and discipline which they practised in the erection of the many sacred edifices in which they were engaged. A portion of these ceremonial usages and of this discipline he would naturally be inclined to introduce among the workmen at Jerusalem. He therefore united them in a society, similar in many respects to that of the Dionysiac artificers. He inculcated lessons of charity and brotherly love; he established a ceremony of initiation, to test experimentally the fortitude and worth of the candidate; adopted modes of recognition; and impressed the obligations of duty and principles of morality by means of symbols and allegories.

To the laborers and men of burden, the Ish Sabal, and to the craftsmen, corresponding with the first and second degrees of more modern Masonry, but little secret knowledge was confided. Like the aspirants in the lesser Mysteries of paganism, their instructions were simply to purify and prepare them for a more solemn ordeal, and for the knowledge of the sublimest truths. These were to be found only in the Master's degree, which it was intended should be in imitation of the greater Mysteries; and in it were to be unfolded, explained, and enforced the great doctrines of the unity of God and the immortality of the soul. But here there must have at once arisen an apparently insurmountable obstacle to the further continuation of the resemblance of Masonry to the Mysteries of Dionysus. In the pagan Mysteries, I have already said that these lessons were allegorically taught by means of a legend. Now, in the Mysteries of Dionysus, the legend was that of the death and subsequent resuscitation of the god Dionysus. But it would have been utterly impossible to introduce such a legend as the basis of any instructions to be communicated to Jewish candidates. Any allusion to the mythological fables of their Gentile neighbors, any celebration of the myths of pagan theology, would have been equally offensive to the taste and repugnant to the religious prejudices of a nation educated, from generation to generation, in the worship of a divine being jealous of his prerogatives, and who had made himself known to his people as the JEHOVAH, the God of time present, past, and future. How this obstacle would have been surmounted by the Israelitish founder of the order I am unable to say: a substitute would, no doubt, have been invented, which would have met all the symbolic requirements of the legend of the Mysteries, or Spurious Freemasonry, without violating the religious principles of the Primitive Freemasonry of the Jews; but the necessity for such invention never existed, and before the completion of the temple a melancholy event is said to have occurred, which served to cut the Gordian knot, and the death of its chief architect has supplied Freemasonry with its appropriate legend—a legend which, like the legends of all the Mysteries, is used to testify our faith in the resurrection of the body and the immortality of the soul.

Before concluding this part of the subject, it is proper that something should be said of the authenticity of the legend of the third degree. Some distinguished Masons are disposed to give it full credence as an historical fact, while others look upon it only as a beautiful allegory. So far as the question has any bearing upon the symbolism of Freemasonry it is not of importance; but those who contend for its historical character assert that they do so on the following grounds:—

First. Because the character of the legend is such as to meet all the requirements of the well-known axiom of Vincentius Lirinensis, as to what we are to believe in traditionary matters.

"Quod semper, quod ubique, quod ab omnibus traditum est."

That is, we are to believe whatever tradition has been at all times, in all places, and by all persons handed down.

With this rule the legend of Hiram Abif, they say, agrees in every respect. It has been universally received, and almost universally credited, among Freemasons from the earliest times. We have no record of any Masonry having ever existed since the time of the temple without it; and, indeed, it is so closely interwoven into the whole system, forming the most essential part of it, and giving it its most determinative character, that it is evident that the institution could no more exist without the legend, than the legend could have been retained without the institution. This, therefore, the advocates of the historical character of the legend think, gives probability at least to its truth.

Secondly. It is not contradicted by the scriptural history of the transactions at the temple, and therefore, in the absence of the only existing written authority on the subject, we are at liberty to depend on traditional information, provided the tradition be, as it is contended that in this instance it is, reasonable, probable, and supported by uninterrupted succession.

Thirdly. It is contended that the very silence of Scripture in relation to the death of Hiram, the Builder, is an argument in favor of the mysterious nature of that death. A man so important in his position as to have been called the favorite of two kings,—sent by one and received by the other as a gift of surpassing value, and the donation thought worthy of a special record, would hardly have passed into oblivion, when his labor was finished, without the memento of a single line, unless his death had taken place in such a way as to render a public account of it improper. And this is supposed to have been the fact. It had become the legend of the new Mysteries, and, like those of the old ones, was only to be divulged when accompanied with the symbolic instructions which it was intended to impress upon the minds of the aspirants.

But if, on the other hand, it be admitted that the legend of the third degree is a fiction,—that the whole masonic and extra-scriptural account of Hiram Abif is simply a myth,—it could not, in the slightest degree, affect the theory which it is my object to establish. For since, in a mythic relation, as the learned Müller has observed, fact and imagination, the real and the ideal, are very closely united, and since the myth itself always arises, according to the same author, out of a necessity and unconsciousness on the part of its framers, and by impulses which act alike on all, we must go back to the Spurious Freemasonry of the Dionysiacs for the principle which led to the involuntary formation of this Hiramic myth; and then we arrive at the same result, which has been already indicated, namely, that the necessity of the religious sentiment in the Jewish mind, to which the introduction of the legend of Dionysus would have been abhorrent, led to the substitution for it of that of Hiram, in which the ideal parts of the narrative have been intimately blended with real transactions. Thus, that there was such a man as Hiram Abif; that he was the chief builder at the temple of Jerusalem; that he was the confidential friend of the kings of Israel and Tyre, which is indicated by his title of *Ab*, or father; and that he is not heard of after the completion of the temple,—are all historical facts. That he died by violence, and in the way described in the masonic legend, may be also true, or may be merely mythical elements incorporated into the historical narrative.

But whether this be so or not,—whether the legend be a fact or a fiction, a history or a myth,—this, at least, is certain: that it was adopted by the Solomonic Masons of the temple as a substitute for the idolatrous legend of the death of Dionysus which belonged to the Dionysiac Mysteries of the Tyrian workmen.

www.ingramcontent.com/pod-product-compliance
Lightning Source LLC
Chambersburg PA
CBHW020355170426
43200CB00005B/180